FIRE EFFECTS PLANNING FRAMEWORK

**United States
Department
of Agriculture**

Forest Service

**Rocky Mountain
Research Station**

**General Technical
Report RMRS-GTR-163WWW**

October 2005

User's Guide
Version 1.0

**Anne E. Black
Tonja Opperman**

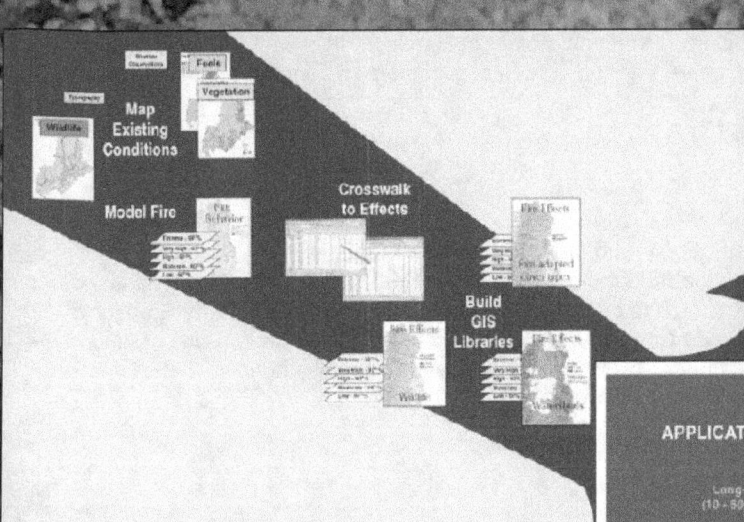

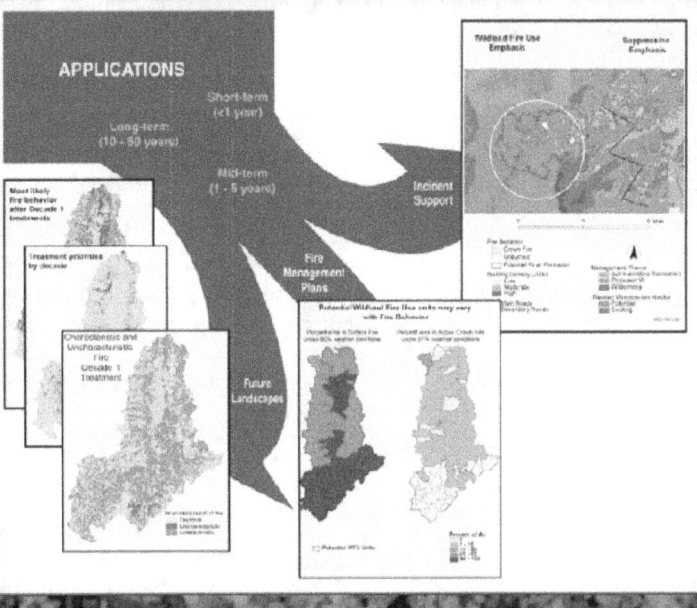

Black, A.; Opperman, T. 2005. **Fire Effects Planning Framework: a user's guide.** Gen. Tech. Rep.GTR-RMRS-163WWW. Fort Colins, CO: U.S. Department of Agriculture, Forest Service, Rocky Mountain Research Station. 63 p.

Abstract

Each decision to suppress fire reinforces a feedback cycle in which fuels continue to accumulate, risk escalates, and the tendency to suppress fires grows (Miller and others, 2003). Existing decision-support tools focus primarily on the negative consequences of fire. This guide outlines a framework managers can use to (1) identify key areas of fire risk and (2) systematically determine where and under what fire weather conditions fire will benefit ecological conditions and management targets while reducing fuels. The Fire Effects Planning Framework (FEPF) sequentially links state-of-the-art, publicly available analysis tools, data, and knowledge to generate GIS-based planning information for a variety of scales. Primary funding for this effort was provided by the Joint Fire Science Program and the National Fire Plan.

Keywords: fire, prescribed fire, wildland fire use, planning, fire effects, fuel treatment priorities, benefits, resource effects, FEPF, GIS, FLAMMAP, SIMPPLLE .

Authors

Anne E. Black is a post-doctoral ecologist with the Rocky Mountain Research Station at the Aldo Leopold Wilderness Research Institute in Missoula, MT. She completed a B.S. degree in resource conservation at the University of Montana's School of Forestry, a Master's degree in Environmental Studies from Yale University, and a Ph.D. in ecology from University of Idaho.

Tonja Opperman is a fire ecologist with the Bitterroot National Forest in Hamilton, MT. She earned a B.S. degree in Forestry from Michigan Technological University and a Master's degree in Forest Science from Yale University.

Acknowledgements

To develop and test this framework, we worked closely with fire and resource managers from a number of different agencies. Key among them are staff from the Bitterroot National Forest, Beaverhead-Deerlodge National Forest, and Yosemite National Park. The guidebook has benefited from the critical reviews of Larry Bradshaw, Deb Tirmenstein and Mark Finney. Jimmie Chew provided advice during analysis. This document was produced as part of a Joint Fire Science Project: "Wildland Fuels: planning and evaluating benefits and risks."

You may order additional copies of this publication by sending your mailing information in label form through one of the following media. Please specify the publication title and series number.

Fort Collins Service Center

Telephone	(970) 498-1392
FAX	(970) 498-1396
E-mail	rschneider@fs.fed.us
Web site	http://www.fs.fed.us/rm
Mailing address	Publications Distribution
	Rocky Mountain Research Station
	240 West Prospect Road
	Fort Collins, CO 80526

Rocky Mountain Research Station
Natural Resources Research Center
2150 Centre Avenue, Building A
Fort Collins, CO 80526

Fire Effects Planning Framework: Users Guide
Table of Contents

List of Figures

I. The Fire Effects Planning Framework

Summary

Each decision to suppress fire reinforces a feedback cycle in which fuels continue to accumulate, risk escalates, and the tendency to suppress fires grows (Miller and others 2004). To make good decisions regarding fuels and fire, managers need to assess the benefits, risks, and consequences of fire and fire suppression. Without information on the benefits of fire, justifying wildland fire as a management strategy may be unpractical. The need for information is immediate, but existing decision-support tools focus primarily on the negative consequences of fire.

The challenge, then, is to create and institutionalize a more balanced analysis of fire (fire stewardship), considering both ecological and social benefits and risks. The goal can be facilitated by using tools that managers already have and working within existing planning and activity frameworks (e.g., using fire management and prediction tools to inform resource planning). Information on benefits must be available before major planning efforts (long-range planning, annual Fire Management Plan development, incident management). Additionally, information must be expressed in units that directly translate into those currently used to describe both land and fire management plans.

These needs determined the focus of the Fire Effects Planning Framework (FEPF):
- to allow functional integration of fire and resource tasks;
- to express fire effects in terms meaningful to both fire and resource staff; and
- to enable immediate use by relying on existing tools and knowledge.

The FEPF allows managers to systematically determine (map and quantify) where and under what fire weather conditions fire is likely to create benefits or pose threats to important ecological conditions or management targets. FEPF[1] is not a stand-alone tool; it is more of a conceptual model or 'meta-model' that sequentially links state-of-the-art, publicly available analysis tools, data, and knowledge to generate information for a variety of planning scales from long-range to site-specific. The key is to develop this information in the off-season and have it available in digital and/or hard copy form for decision-makers during the fire season.

The process outlined by FEPF is straightforward (**Figure 1**):

- Map existing conditions of each planning target (fish and wildlife, vegetative condition, fuels, firefighter safety, and so forth);

---

[1] FEPF does not provide special software; rather it outlines an analysis process using existing software to support strategic and tactical fire planning.

- Model fire;
- Identify how various fire behaviors (for example, surface vs. crown fire) are likely to affect targeted resources (causing a move towards or away from desired condition) and capture this in database 'crosswalks';
- Use these crosswalks to build GIS map libraries that display expected effects of fire on social and ecological values; and
- Use the resulting map libraries to:
  - Assist in long-range planning, for instance to help analyze alternative management strategies;
  - Assist in mid-range planning such as developing Fire Management Plans to identify potential Wildland Fire Use zones and prescriptions for the go/no-go decision;
  - Assist incident support, for instance to identify where fire is likely to provide benefits or pose risks to planning targets;
  - Quantify the cumulative effect of a fire season on long-range planning targets;
  - Identify treatment priorities for the next season; and
  - Determine feasibility of wildland fire use (WFU), prescribed fire (Rx), mechanical treatment, or suppression.

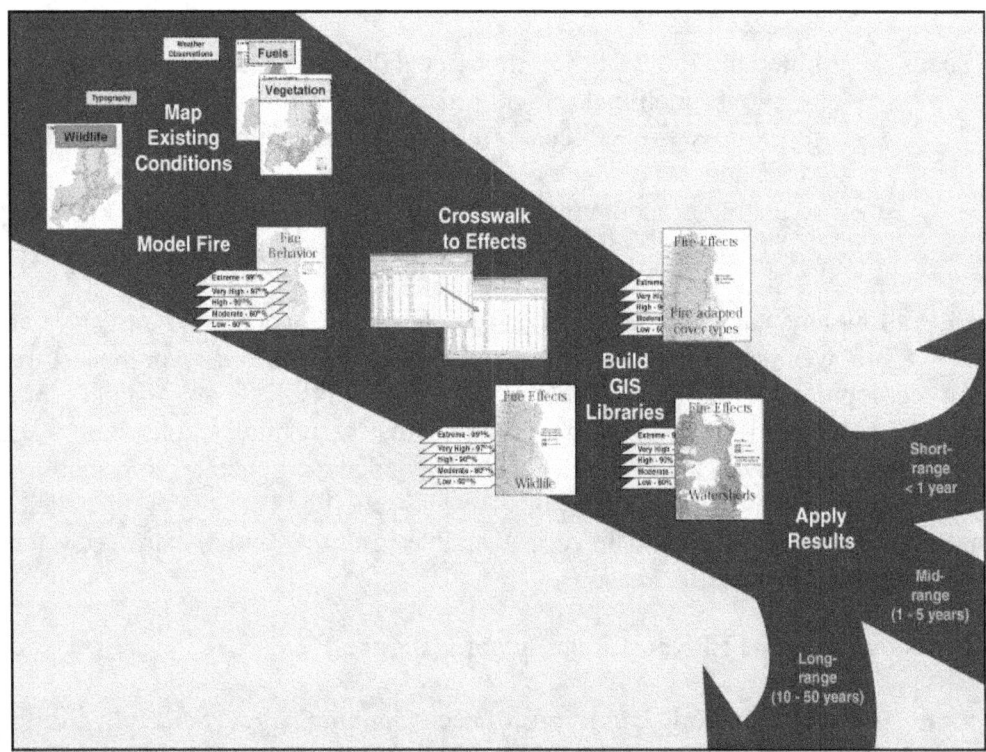

Figure 1 - Basic elements of the Fire Effects Planning Framework process.

One can operationalize FEPF in many ways and build numerous tools into the framework. In this guide we describe the framework and then illustrate the process using examples of both stand-based and landscape-level models. We take advantage of models currently in use by regional fire and resource planners (FLAMMAP and SIMPPLLE, respectively). We do not claim that these are the 'best' tools for determining benefits and risk; they are simply two models available now. Where tools are unavailable, others may be substituted. Readers from these areas may still benefit from the overview and procedural descriptions included in this guide. This guide is not intended to replace the user's guides or courses supporting individual programs that FEPF draws upon; instead, we offer it as a means to integrate existing programs to provide information none provide alone.

As with any analysis it is important to keep in mind key limitations of the models used. All models are simplifications of reality; none provides an infallible or complete picture of the real world. Fire effects as predicted by the tools used here reflect current knowledge of fire effects predominantly on above-ground biomass. They also assume that fuels are homogeneous within a mapped unit – be that a polygon or a pixel. At this time, we – as a management and scientific community – lack the ability to quantify, predict and spatially display ground[2] fuels, ground fire behavior, or ground fire effects[3]. Thus, it is not possible in 2005 to accurately and consistently predict effects on soils at a landscape level, or to quantitatively predict whether a 'surface' fire is likely to result in stand replacement of fire tolerant species due to ground fuel accumulation and consumption. (As new information and new models become available, they can be readily incorporated into FEPF.)

Management Questions Addressed by FEPF

FEPF produces information on the relative risks and benefits of fire under a variety of different conditions. Benefits and risks may be monetary or non-monetary. Monetary benefits are most likely to result from reduced cost of future management or fire suppression efforts than from the sale of a commodity. We focus on non-monetary benefits and risks. We define benefit as the number of acres that will be moved towards or into a more desirable condition based on reference to the area's targets found in long-range plans, Fire Management Plans, monitoring plans, and other targets such as management indicator species. Risks are defined as undesirable effects resulting from movement away from target conditions.

FEPF's output units are the same as those used by resource managers to track ecosystem targets and by fire managers to evaluate fire behavior (for example, habitat or fuels). Resulting spatially explicit map libraries can support fire management decisions at many strategic levels (**Figure 2**):

---

[2] Ground fire is defined as fire in the upper, organic layers of the soil horizon, as distinct from surface fire which burns fuels on top of the soil and in the grass and shrub layer (see DeBano or Agee).
[3] However, FOFEM5.0 begins to address this important issue.

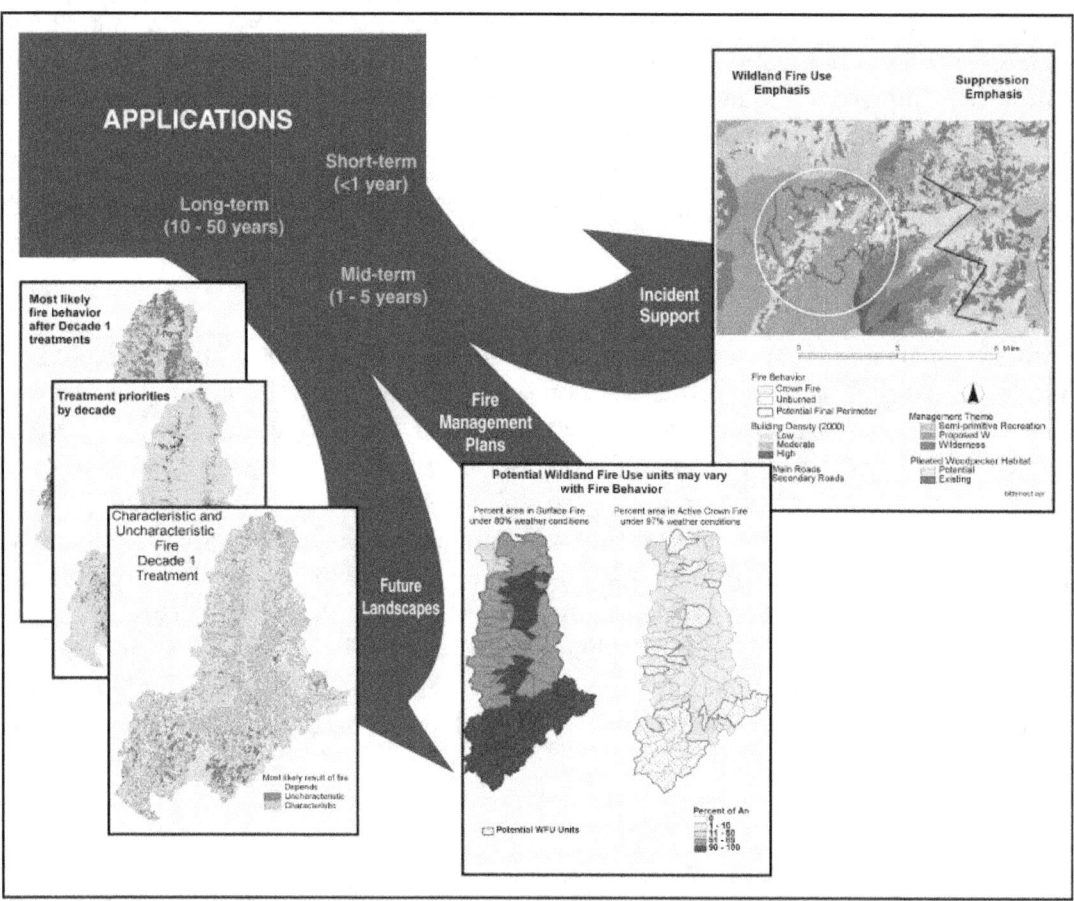

Figure 2 – Applications of Fire Effects Planning Framework output.

- *Planning* (long-term, broad-scale): prediction, quantification, and mapping of ability to meet future planning targets under proposed and alternative fire management strategies. Includes monitoring and reporting of progress.
  - How are proposed fire management tactics (suppression, prescribed fire, wildland fire use) likely to influence our ability to meet proposed resource targets in specific areas?

- *Fire management plan* (mid-term, broad-scale): delineation of wildland fire use (WFU) fire management units derived from benefit/risk maps.
  - Under particular weather conditions (for example, 80th percentile ERC), where are there opportunities for WFU or prescribed fire?

- *Fuels treatment* (short to mid-term, fine-scale): identification and prioritization of areas (a) where treatment by fire (Rx or WFU) would assist in meeting planning targets, and (b) where mechanical treatment is preferred from a fire behavior or ecological perspective.
  - Where are fuel conditions such that mechanical treatments should be used before reintroduction/application of fire?

- *Incident Support* (short-term, fine-scale): identification and quantification of ecological benefits, such as changes in habitat or fuel profiles, for development of Wildland Fire Implementation Planning (WFIP) Stage I, II, or III, and Wildland Fire Situation Analyses (WFSA); identification of areas where light-handed suppression techniques may be most appropriate from ecological and cost-containment perspectives.

- Where are opportunities for accomplishing resource objectives, lowering costs of fire management, or creating fuel breaks for populated areas or areas of potentially severe fire behavior?

Model Considerations

Ideally, FEPF would rest upon a model, or suite of models, that provide quantitative measures of the contagious processes involved in succession and disturbance (fire, disease, fuels, vegetation growth, and management) across the entire western United States. Unfortunately, although a rich variety of models is currently available, none can 'do it all'. Because users must choose from among existing models to populate FEPF, users should understand something about the strengths and weaknesses of models. Our intent in this section is not to provide a comprehensive review of models – that is covered elsewhere (see for instance Barrett 2001, Lee and others 2003) – but to raise a couple of basic differentiations users should consider before initiating analysis: contagion and variability.

In general, the choice of model to incorporate into FEPF is between a deterministic, stand-based model and a stochastic, landscape-based model. Landscape-level models (or landscape dynamic simulation models, LDSMs) explicitly incorporate spread[4] into the determination of stand conditions. Most LDSMs are stochastic, producing multiple outcomes for a given set of inputs by varying the inputs according to some distribution. The distribution is often an estimation of natural variability. The advantage is that incorporation of both experimental and experiential knowledge allows construction of complex and often comprehensive system models. A key disadvantage is that it is not possible to calculate significance or error measures for those parts of the model based on expert opinion, and it is difficult to evaluate how closely predictions will emulate the actual future.

Alternatively, stand-level models do not account for spread between stands but can often be mapped spatially. Most stand-level models are deterministic. They produce a single outcome for a given set of inputs. Their advantage is that the significance and error associated with the experimental data are known. Their main weakness is that they must often greatly simplify the ecological processes of interest, incorporating only those pieces that can be measured and controlled in an experiment. For both types of models, it is difficult to disentangle error from variability. Further, when working with any type of model, one must remember to treat results only as indicators of reality.

---

[4] Spread, or contagion, refers to whether what is adjacent has an impact on behavior or processes within each polygon (stand) or pixel.

To determine which type of model best suits the user's needs for FEPF, consider these questions:

- Where are you most comfortable accepting error/variability:
  - incorporated into the outcome → use a stochastic model, or
  - excluded from the outcome → use a deterministic model?

- Do you desire a quantitative measure
  - of error → possible for deterministic models, or
  - of variability → possible for stochastic models?

- Is your primary interest
  - to develop information about the current situation → either, or
  - to compare results of alternative management strategies → stochastic?

- How important is spread:
  - can you accept stand-based predictions (no spread), or
  - do you need to consider the influence of spread?

We describe how to use FEPF with two models: a deterministic, stand-based model (FLAMMAP, Finney, in press), and a stochastic, landscape model (SIMPPLLE, Chew and others 2004, Chew 1995). Though both are spatial, they have very different architectures. Briefly, FLAMMAP is a non-contagious, deterministic program based on empirically-derived fire process/behavior equations (for example, Rothermel's [1972] and Albini's [1976] fire behavior equations).While it maps fire behavior across an entire landscape, calculations are performed on each pixel independently. FLAMMAP uses quantified fuels information for a single point in time. To enable consideration of future fire behavior, a vegetation simulator must be used to create future fuels data. Because FLAMMAP is based on process equations, it is easily transported to any situation in which base data on vegetation and fuels are available. SIMPPLLE is a stochastic, contagious vegetation dynamics simulator developed from both empirical and knowledge-based sources. It incorporates significant process variability (climate, fire weather, suppression efficiency, fire start location) and calculates fire effects by considering biophysical and vegetative conditions in both the 'initiating' and 'receiving' polygons/pixels. SIMPPLLE does not generate or track quantitative fuels information, but because it incorporates fire effects, it can be used to model either the current or future situations. Because SIMPPLLE incorporates significant local information about a number of complex ecosystem processes (insects, disease, fire) which science has yet to define or describe mathematically at the landscape scale, SIMPPLLE must be parameterized locally (generally by forest or region, BLM Resource Area, or planning unit)[5].

We do not recommend use or avoidance of any particular model; nor will following this protocol provide a black-box that will give you the 'right' answer. Following the Framework will provide you with information relevant to your area and be useful to both fire and resource management to aid in decision-making.

---

[5] SIMPPLLE datasets have been created and parameterized for a number of National Forests and BLM Resource Areas around the west, predominantly in the Northern Rockies, but including southern California, the Kenai and Michigan's Upper Peninsula (Chew and others 2004).

Software, Skills and Data Requirements

Software

FEPF requires several existing **software** programs. For all versions of the analysis, a spatial mapping program – such as ARCVIEW or ARCGIS – is required.

To develop map libraries of fire behavior and fire effects programs :
- FIREFAMILYPLUS – to generate weather stream information for FLAMMAP;
- FLAMMAP – to generate fire behavior maps; and
- FARSITE – to generate weather files from the FIREFAMILYPLUS analysis.

To generate information on potential future landscapes, or to consider current conditions from a landscape perspective, you will also need a landscape dynamic simulation model (LDSM). For this document, we used
- SIMPPLLE, but are currently working with FVS-FFE as well. Other LDSMs, such as LANDSUM or RMLANDS, may also be used.

To generate other fire effects, we used FOFEM for emissions and first order fire effects such as mineral soil exposed or soil heating. One can also build in sedimentation or run-off models. Disturbed-WEPP is an existing stand-based model.

With the exception of the ESRI products (ARCVIEW, ARCGIS), all may be downloaded from the Internet at no cost (visit www.frames.gov, SIMPPLLE site). ESRI products are proprietary and should be obtained from your IT specialist. Contact the SIMPPLLE developers group (Chew and others 2004) to determine whether SIMPLLE is available for your area.

Skills, expertise and time

While this guide is intended for both expert and casual users of the identified software programs, a basic understanding of the tools is assumed. Although the fire-related tools are easier to use "out of the box" than ESRI products (the ARC suite), consultation with fire experts is recommended to ensure proper identification of key parameters and model specification. Information in the detailed TASK sections provide tips on how to accomplish each ACTION and assists in methodological consistency and documentation.

The most time-consuming aspect of FEPF – and the one requiring coordination among the most people – is likely to be specification of fire effects. In the absence of comprehensive knowledge of fire effects based on experimental results, much of the information to build the fire behavior – fire effects crosswalks – will need to be inferred from available models, literature, and local knowledge. These crosswalks should be developed with or reviewed by relevant experts.

Data

FEPF input data are those required and/or developed during land management planning activities: GIS data on vegetation, fuels, fire weather, fire occurrence, and hydrology, and resource targets for fisheries, wildlife, recreation and silvics, and so forth. The models we've used to operationalize FEPF will require manipulation of these general datasets as outlined below.

To develop **planning target** maps, you will need to identify characteristics of the target that can be linked to GIS map attributes (of vegetative, soils, and/or aquatic condition).

To develop **fire behavior** maps with FLAMMAP you will need:

- *Daily fire weather data.* Daily weather data is processed through FIREFAMILYPLUS to identify fire behavior parameters, such as Energy Release Component (ERC) values, at threshold fire weather conditions (for example, $80^{th}\%$, $90^{th}\%$, $97^{th}\%$, or $99^{th}\%$). This information is then used to produce wind and weather files for FLAMMAP.
- *Digital DEM and fuels data.* These include the necessary GIS grids to create a FLAMMAP landscape file (.lcp): fire behavior fuel model, canopy fuels data (stand height, crown closure, crown base height, crown bulk density); and digital elevation models for calculating separate grids of aspect, slope, and elevation.

To develop **probability of fire, of fire type,** and **of return interval,** using SIMPPLLE, you will need, in addition to a modified existing vegetation cover and a series of parameter files for ecosystem processes (fire, insects/disease, succession):

- *Historic fire starts.* This cover is used to determine appropriate number of starts per simulation time step.
- *Fire Management Units (or fire management zones, whichever is used for tactical decisions).* This cover is used in combination with the historic start information to determine how to distribute starts spatially. Though a fire management zone map is most often used, one could just as easily use an ecologically based map such as Potential Vegetation Type to distribute fire starts. This cover can also be used to calculate suppression costs.
- *Land use.* The FMU/FMZ or Land Use cover is used to specify type of fire management strategy (for example, Wildland Fire Use) and fire suppression efficiency rates.

To develop a map library of **fire effects**, you will need, in addition to the vegetation cover:

- *Ancillary resource data.* Additional data are used to predict probable locations of management indicators or resource targets. Examples might be aspect, elevation, soils, or aquatic data.

II. Guide to FEPF Using Demonstrated Models

How to Use This Guide

This guide is broken into two main sections: an overview of FEPF (above), and a guide to FEPF. The following guide is broken into three chapters covering: (1) development of crosswalks, (2) development of map libraries, and (3) use of map libraries. Chapter 2 contains four non-sequential sub-sections outlining development of map libraries for current and future conditions using both a stand- and a landscape-based model. Which sub-section you choose in Chapter 2 depends on the type of analysis you wish to perform and the model assumptions you are willing to accept:

- current condition analysis using a stand-based, deterministic model; → 2A
- current condition analysis using a landscape-level, stochastic model; → 2B
- future condition analysis using a stand-based, deterministic model; → 2C
- future condition analysis using a landscape-level, stochastic model → 2D

Within each chapter, we describe the Framework using three headings with an increasing order of detail - **ACTION, DISCUSSION, TASKS** - to assist users of various skill levels. This guide also provides a number of FORMS to assist in planning and tracking analyses. EXAMPLES are offered to illustrate the **ACTION**.

ACTION briefly identifies the task and outcome of the section. Users who have already generated this information or know how to use the programs utilized in the step can skip ahead to the next **ACTION**. Such users may still be interested in reading the discussion section to ensure that their existing data, or alternative method, include the information necessary in future steps. Information included under this section should also be helpful in determining how outcomes might differ if alternative processes are used.

DISCUSSION provides background on the goal of the action and identifies some of the alternatives and key assumptions.

TASKS provide a more detailed step-by-step guide to generate the outcome using specified computer models or programs. This subsection is intended as a mechanical guide to supplement the existing user's guide for each program; it does *not* substitute for consultation with the relevant expert or for training on the programs. Generation of each outcome may require consultation with local experts to determine parameters of interest, thresholds, and data sources.

The FORMS subsection offers forms we have developed for collecting or evaluating input data.

We supplement the guide with sidebars using examples from our work on the Bitterroot National Forest.

Chapter 1. Developing rule-sets (crosswalks) to link fire behavior to fire effects for each management target

FEPF uses effects of fire on ecosystem targets (for example, management goals or Desired Future Conditions/processes) as the criteria for evaluating the desirability of fire. This is calculated in a spatial context to allow easy quantification of benefits and risks and because many targets contain spatial criteria. Thus, it is important to be able to link some critical aspect of the target or ecological process to a map-attribute affected by fire: vegetation, soils, water.

Linkage of fire behavior to fire effects rests on the development of rule-sets, or crosswalks. We found it helpful to break these crosswalks down into logical steps, first assessing effects to vegetation, then basing species effects assessments on changes in vegetation, and finally determining whether these changes are a benefit – movement towards the desired condition, or a risk – movement away from target conditions. Following this logic, you will need to develop several crosswalks, which may be combined into a single crosswalk upon completion (**Figure 3**):

> (1) An initial crosswalk to identify how to map management targets spatially using available data (for example, use a species-habitat relationship to map a species).
> (2) Another to identify how fire of various intensities/severities affects the primary dataset (generally vegetation for terrestrial species, soils for sedimentation/erosion processes, and/or aquatic for aquatic species) – first-order.
> (3) In some cases, you can use the initial crosswalk (1) to determine fire effect, but for many species, you will need a third crosswalk to translate the first-order effects into second order habitat effects.
> (4) A fourth crosswalk may be necessary to specify how changes in habitat will affect the target.
> (5) A final crosswalk containing the rules used to determine whether fire will confer a benefit or a risk.

These steps should be repeated for each target. Sources of information for determining most likely fire effects can be obtained from local expert knowledge, quantified from previous fires, or predicted from other computer tools such as FOFEM or SIMPPLLE. Confidence in the final maps, and in the plans based on these maps, will increase if appropriate planning and resource staff is included in this step of the process.

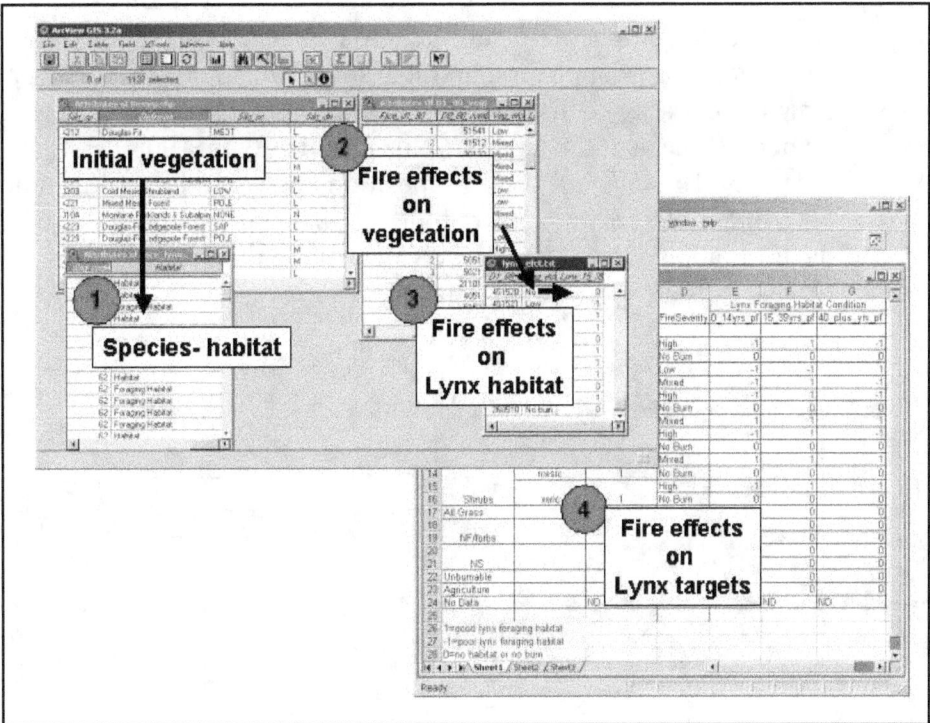

Figure 3 – Crosswalk needed to determine fire effects.

Map Ecosystem Targets or Processes

DISCUSSION: To ensure easy updating and defensible cross-walks (science-based and transparent), base the mapping criteria on parameters and attributes contained in pre-existing digital vegetation (GIS) data. For instance, if you have an understory-nesting bird species and a vegetation cover that maps only cover type and 'Habitat Type', consider using the 'Habitat Type' attribute if you can point to peer-reviewed literature that identifies the particular understory conditions required by the bird species as being present in specific habitat types. Clearly identify the relevant ecological and scientific basis of the link between the target and map attributes and store this in a new text (string) attribute.

TASKS

1. Create a 'join' field in your GIS vegetation layer and create a 'primary ecosystem component' field (**Figure 4**). Calculate this field as a concatenation of the individual vegetation attributes (for example, cover type, size class, density, height). This field should be calculated in the baseline dataset and in any future simulation sets. This will be one of your primary 'join' fields. Once created, changes in either fire behavior or vegetation structure are easily re-mapped into new effects maps using this crosswalk. For targets that respond

most closely to fire-related changes in soils or water, complete this step for those baseline datasets as well.

1.1. Count the number of classes of each attribute and determine the appropriate multiple of 10 sufficient to enable concatenation into a unique descriptor. For example, in our dataset, we had 12 classes of cover type, 8 structure classes, 4 densities and 3 stand height classes. We created a numeric value as follows: new value = (cover type*10000 + structure*100 + density*10). (We left the ones position open to multiply this unique descriptor "<FLAMMAP grid output variable>*1" in a later step.) Capture the translation of text to numeric values in text files (.txt).

1.2. Create the new field and populate it.

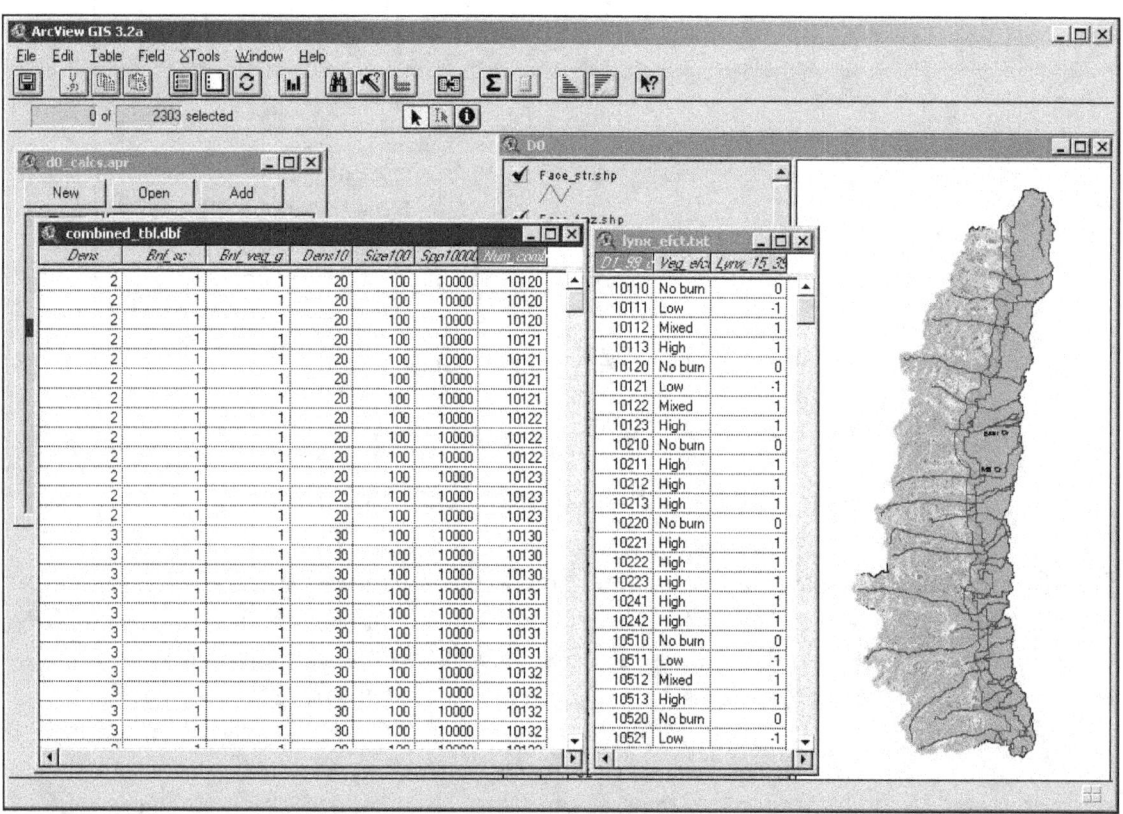

Figure 4 - Illustration of concatenation field and join tables.

Define Fire Effects on Ecosystem Targets or Processes

DISCUSSION: This is generally a two step process, first to identify how fire is likely to affect the vegetation (or soils, water), then how these changes will affect the target of interest.

STEP 1. Define how various fire behaviors are likely to affect the primary ecosystem component _____

TASKS

1. Create a .txt file (or table) identifying how the various fire behavior classes you will use are likely to affect the primary ecosystem component. For example, if using the crown fire potential option in FLAMMAP, is a surface fire likely to be light, moderate, or stand-replacing in a stand of sapling sub-alpine fir?

STEP 2. Define how the resulting changes in the primary ecosystem component is likely to affect each target _____

TASKS

1. Create a .txt file (or table) identifying how change in the primary ecosystem component is likely to affect each target. For example, is moderate severity fire in a stand of sapling sub-alpine fir likely increase or decrease habitat quality for the target species?
2. (If necessary) specify additional spatial and/or temporal criteria crosswalks.

Define Risk and Benefit

Benefits and risks may be identified for a single time-step (FLAMMAP, SIMPPLLE), under particular weather conditions (FLAMMAP), or compared across different management scenarios (SIMPPLLE).

ACTION: Determine whether changes in each target are a benefit or a risk. This determination will depend upon your targets and the basis for those targets. For instance, if your goal is to manage a resource within a certain 'range of variability', then you may need only 2 classes – a 'desirable' or 'characteristic' class that is interpreted as a benefit, and an 'undesirable' or 'uncharacteristic' class that is a risk. If there is a greater range of effects – or additional criteria, such as patch size, you may need additional classes to adequately assess risk or benefit.

TASKS

1. Create a .txt file (or table) identifying whether the change in the target assists in meeting long-term planning targets (benefit) or inhibits attainment (risk). For example, is a decrease in habitat quality for the target species acceptable?

SIDEBAR 1: Determining fire effects on lynx on the Bitterroot National Forest

Step 1. Map existing lynx habitat.

Based on the Lynx Conservation Assessment Strategy and discussions with biologists on the Bitterroot National Forest, we defined critical habitat as lynx foraging habitat. Foraging habitat in this area consists of 15-45 year old stands of trees above 6200' elevation (Ruediger and others, 2000). Since we did not have stand age in our vegetation data, but did have structure, we used stand dynamics information to determine that sapling and pole size classes meet the age criteria. We combined these criteria to map existing lynx foraging habitat.

Step 2. Create a crosswalk between fire behavior and vegetation effects.

We knew we would use Crown Fire Potential as our measure of fire behavior for modeling effects on lynx. FLAMMAP identifies four classes in its prediction of crown fire potential (no fire, surface fire, passive crown fire, and active crown fire). This crosswalk consists of three columns: the primary ecosystem component (our combined numeric value describing all four vegetation characteristics), the four fire types, and a final column to hold our vegetation effect. For instance, we focused on fire types resulting in stand replacement within lynx foraging habitat.

Step 3. Create a crosswalk between vegetation effects and lynx foraging habitat.

Lynx foraging habitat develops 15-39 years post-fire in conifer habitats at the proper elevations. This simple crosswalk identified which of the combinations in Step 2 met this criteria.

Step 4. Identify fire and habitat effects desirable and undesirable for lynx.

Stand replacing fire in current foraging habitat removes lynx habitat for up to 15 years. Stands older than 45 years no longer provide foraging habitat and in these areas a stand replacing fire will create future habitat. If the key concern is current foraging habitat, then a stand-replacing fire in existing habitat is undesirable and the creation of future habitat may be neutral. If the concern is to maximize habitat in the future, then fire may be a benefit in both. An additional 'rule' or crosswalk might consider either the spatial arrangement of foraging habitat or the proportion of habitat desired in each Lynx Assessment Unit. In this last case, the target might be a certain proportion of area in habitat and the measure of risk or benefit would be whether fire is likely to move the unit towards or away from that target.

Chapter 2. Creating map libraries for analysis of ...

This chapter is broken into four non-sequential subsections. Choose whichever subsection corresponds to the time-scale of primary interest and the model type you're using:

A. Current conditions analysis using a stand-based, deterministic model;
B. Current condition analysis using a landscape-level, stochastic model;
C. Future condition analysis using a stand-based, deterministic model; or
D. Future condition analysis using a landscape-level, stochastic model.

A

Current Conditions Using a Stand-based, Deterministic Model

This section outlines the development of map libraries of fire behavior using a stand-based, deterministic model (**Figure 5**). The goal is to predict fire behavior under a suite of fire weather conditions meaningful for fire management. You will need to identify and use a fire behavior metric (for example, Energy Release Component) and percentile weather thresholds (such as 80%, 90%, 99%) used by local fire officials for strategic and tactical decision-making. Hopefully the parameters chosen are the same as those in your Fire Management Plan (FMP). FLAMMAP provides the opportunity to predict a number of fire behavior parameters: crown fire activity, flame length, fire line intensity, heat per unit area, and so forth. We chose to use Crown Fire Activity (CFR) because effects on our ecological targets can be tied to changes in vegetation. For watershed effects one may want to choose heat per unit area (HPA) or other output that can be used to determine effects on soil or aquatic systems more directly.

We use FLAMMAP (FLAMMAP2 , http://fire.org) as our primary model, FIREFAMILYPLUS to summarize and identify threshold weather conditions, FARSITE to generate the wind and weather files, and either FARSITE or FLAMMAP to create the landscape file required by FLAMMAP.

Step 1. Generating the landscape input file _____

ACTION: Use FLAMMAP (or FARSITE) to generate the landscape file (.lcp).

DISCUSSION: Due to the memory requirements of FLAMMAP, it may be necessary to break large geographic areas into smaller sections, generate separate FLAMMAP output for each, then merge the sections in ARC.

All input GIS layers must have the same extent. Clipping all with the same boundary achieves this. For this protocol, you must also have the four canopy fuels data layers (stand height, crown base height, canopy cover, crown bulk density).

TASKS
    1. Create a landscape file (.lcp).

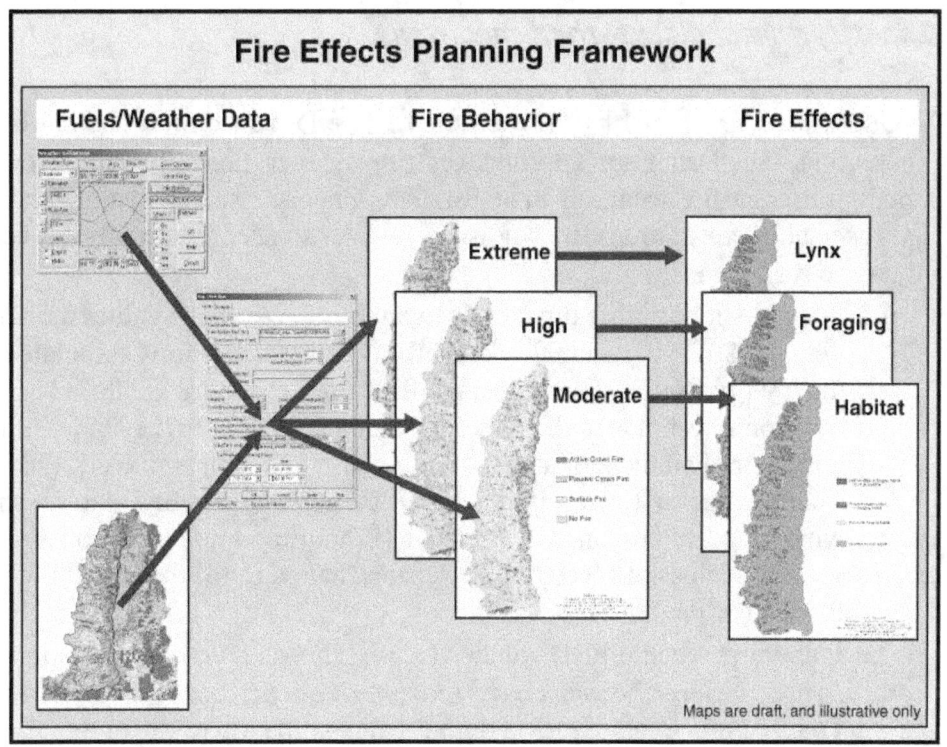

Figure 5 - Overview of **A** current conditions using a stand-based deterministic model.

Step 2. Generating fire weather input files _____

ACTION: Use historical weather data (in FIREFAMILYPLUS and/or Excel) to generate weather input files.

DISCUSSION: To define the typical threshold conditions relevant to any fire year, you will need to determine the appropriate temporal range of fire weather analysis. FLAMMAP uses daily weather data, so the question becomes over what range should threshold values be calculated – weeks, months, years? You may want to consider making some preliminary runs using different analyses to determine the appropriate temporal frame for your analyses. In our studies, we compared FLAMMAP outcomes using a variety of different criteria: separate analyses by month, a single analysis for the entire fire season, and separate analyses for wet/cool, hot/dry, and normal years. For the Bitterroot National Forest, the outcomes were not highly variable; therefore we chose to calculate threshold weather conditions based on the entire fire season.

For each landscape modeled, consult with local fire experts to determine the most appropriate weather stations to use and the areas over which they apply. For instance, on the Bitterroot National Forest, we determined that fire weather and behavior across the forest was sufficiently different to warrant using different weather stations to model different areas – a SIG file combining all weather stations for application across the entire forest was inappropriate.

2.1 Identify threshold weather conditions
TASKS

1. Use FIREFAMILY PLUS (FF+) to complete the Data Form found at the end of this section. The Data Form captures key fire weather threshold values for running different fire scenarios in FLAMMAP. Choose a single weather station or SIG (special interest group) file, and specify dates to use in the analysis (years, months, days).

1.1 Identify fire weather thresholds to analyze. We chose values associated with the 80th, 90th, and 99th percentile weather conditions associated with the Energy Release Component (ERC) since these are identified as decision thresholds in the Fire Management Plan. On the Data Form under Fire Parameter Values, use one box for each parameter. For example, the first box might be for ERC percentile values, the second for wind speed values, and the third for 10-hour total live fuel moisture (TLFM) values. Proceed with the steps below to fill the percentile values for each of the boxes.

1.2 Identify percentile ERC values. In FF+ choose *Weather →Season Reports →Severity Summary →ERC →critical percentile of 80 →Greater Than →Run*. Read the ERC output value at the top of the output, "…percentile values greater than x" and record this number on the Data Form under Fire Parameter Values, 80th percentile. There is no need to save anything else in the output. Repeat this task for 90th and 99th percentiles and record on the form. At the end of task 1.2 you should have three numbers recorded in one of the Data Form boxes under the Fire Parameter Values heading.

1.3 Identify percentile wind speed. In FF+ choose *Weather →Season Reports →Severity Summary →Windspeed → critical percentile of 80 →Greater Than →Run*. Read the wind speed value at the top of the output, "…percentile values greater than x" and record this number for 80th percentile; repeat for 90th and 99th percentile wind speeds. At the end of task 1.3 you should have a number recorded for each percentile of interest in one of the Data Form boxes under the Fire Parameter Values heading. Repeat step 1.3 if you want to obtain 1-hour and 10-hour fuel moisture values independently from ERC (since there is likely little correlation between ERC thresholds and fine fuel moistures).

1.4 Generate fuel moisture and weather values. In FF+ choose *Weather →Season Reports →Daily Listing*. In the dialogue box, select formats MM/DD/YYYY and HH:MM. Leave all other defaults in the top half of the box. Under "Available Variables" choose all the variables you may want to use in your analysis. We chose ERC, wind speed, all fuel moisture parameters (1,10, 100, 1000), precipitation, minimum and maximum temperature, minimum and maximum RH, herbaceous and woody fuel moistures, state of the weather, and wind direction. Press OK at bottom of dialogue box. Save output as *.txt file, and during the next step be sure not to delete any data in this file as it is used differently in two independent tasks.

1.5 Calculate percentile values for each fuel moisture and weather value. In MS Excel, open the *.txt, separate date into three columns, and determine average values for different weather parameters by percentile to use in the FLAMMAP simulation. Do this by opening the *.txt document as a fixed width file in Excel, adjusting columns, and sorting by ERC. Using the ERC threshold values from task 1.2, determine averages for weather values. For example, if 80th percentile threshold is 27, and 90th percentile threshold is 32, take all the ERC values in the Excel spreadsheet from 27 to 31 and average these values to get final parameters for min/max temperature, min/max RH, and fuel moistures of choice. Because ERC does not consider wind, we did not use ERC thresholds to calculate these variables. Repeat for all percentiles.

1.6 To determine values for wind speed, the maximum value is recorded on the Data Form by taking the same *.txt file and sorting it by wind speed. Using the threshold values determined in task 1.3, again parse out the data into sections representing the 80th, 90th, and 99th percentiles. Here, rather than use the average wind speed calculated in these data sets, use the maximum value. Consult with local fire behavior experts to determine if these results are reasonable. Because weather stations only record one wind speed per hour, they can under-characterize winds meaningful to fire behavior (NWS website). We decided to multiply the 90th percentile maximum value by 1.5 and the 99th percentile maximum value by 2.5 to create wind speeds for the final simulation. Repeat for other parameters of interest that are independent of ERC, such as fine fuel values.

2.2 Use threshold weather values to develop FLAMMAP input files
TASKS

1. In FARSITE, choose Input|Define Weather/wind types. An input window will appear (**Figure 6**). (Alternatively, you can use the *Custom* editors, changing values found under *New WTR* and *New WND* files to those of your FireFamilyPlus analysis.)

(a)

(b)

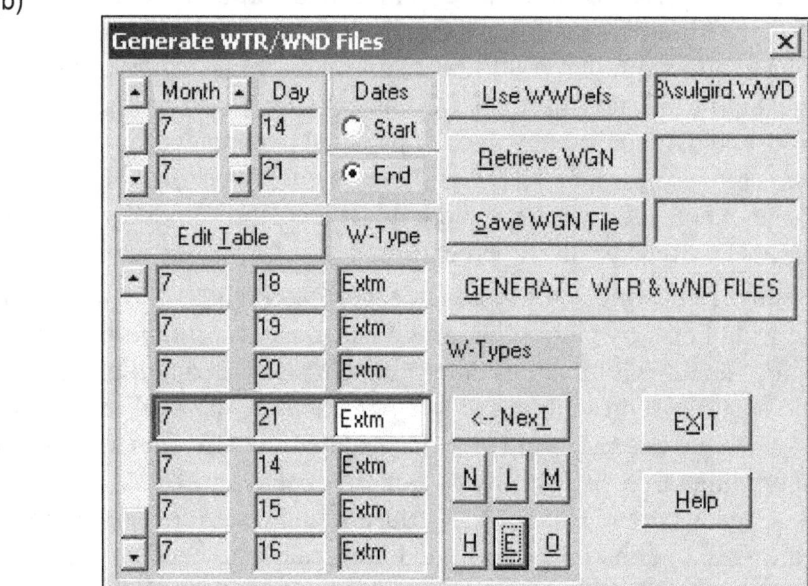

Figure 6 - Generating weather and fuel moisture files for FlamMap.

2. Enter variables relating to each of the adjective ratings (High, Moderate, Low) of interest.

2.1 Select *Weather Type* (for example, Moderate)

2.2 Input *Elevation* from weather station, or average of weather stations used on weather form.

2.3 Set *Rain Amt.* at 0 in.

2.4 Set *T Hi* and *T Lo* and *H Hi* and *H Lo* for this *Weather Type* and the hours when this hi/lo occurs.

2.5 Click on radio button to indicate coarseness of defined winds (we used 4 hours), then click on Wind button to define winds. In this screen, input Wind speed for this "weather type" at the 1200 hr and 1600 hr. Use 0 cloud cover and 0 wind direction (if uphill winds being modeled). Since wind speeds at hours outside of burn period will affect fuel moistures during the conditioning period, input an appropriate number for these hours. We used 2 mph for Moderate weather types during 2000, 2400, 0400, and 0800 hours. We used 4 mph for High and 6 mph for Extreme. This is a judgment call.

2.6 Repeat steps a-e for all other *Weather Types* of interest.

2.7 Save As *.wwd under the Input directory in FLAMMAP where you are storing the files for running this geographic area in FLAMMAP.

3. Use the newly created *.wwd file to generate *.wtr and *.wnd files
in FARSITE :

3.1 In FARSITE, choose *Input|Generate* from types (*.wtr/*.wnd). An input screen will appear.

3.2 Click on Use *WWDefs* button and retrieve *.wwd file.

3.3 Set *Month* and *Day* to set the conditioning period. This should be a full seven days before your intended fire start date. Our fire start date was August 1, so we set start date as July 26 and end date as August 1.

3.4 Click on *Edit Table* to auto-fill dates from above.

3.5 Next, fill in the *W-type* column by clicking on the small square buttons near bottom of input window and the *Nex̲T* button to enter the adjective rating for these wtr/wnd files. For example, we need files created for the "moderate" weather scenario; therefore we click on the "M" and "next" for each day in this conditioning period. Make sure you hit "next" after each entry—especially the final entry.

3.6 The final step is to click on *Generate WTR and WND file*. Enter a filename that will allow you to differentiate this weather condition from others because this step is repeated for each "weather type."

3.7 You should get a FARSITE message indicating that both a .wtr and .wnd file were created.

3.8 Repeat steps a-g for all *Weather Types* that must be generated from this wwd file.

3.9 Repeat steps a-h for additional *.wwd files corresponding to other geographic areas if you have parsed out your landscape.

4. Generate a new initial fuel moisture file (*.fms) file using FARSITE or by editing a default moisture file.

4.1 In FARSITE, go to *Input →Project Inputs* and click on the "→ " to the right of *Moistures (*.fms)*.

4.2 When the dialogue box appears, click the *New .FMS File* button. A new file with fuel models 1-50 and default fuel moistures is displayed in the text box.

4.3 Edit these data based on moisture percentiles on your Data Form. Make sure to include fuel moistures for all fuel models in your .lcp.

4.4 click *Save *.fms file* and save in the directory where your FLAMMAP data are stored.

4.5 Repeat steps a-d for each weather scenario (80th, 90th, and 99th percentiles) and each subunit as needed.

Step 3. Creating a fire behavior library _____

ACTION: Create fire behavior maps for each fire weather threshold.

DISCUSSION: In addition to the input files, you will need to decide and manually set for each FLAMMAP run: wind direction, wind speed, time of burn, fuel conditioning period, and live fuel moisture content. These values will determine conditions for the run, whereas the .fms, .wnd, and .wtr files are used to condition the fuels.

In our demonstrations, we specified *Wind Blowing Uphill*. Based on discussions with Mark Finney (who has found that wind speeds across the western United States – one of the major determinants of crown fire activity – are often 2.5 times those recorded in daily weather streams), we multiplied our 90th percentile winds by 1.5 and 99th percentile winds by 2. We generally specified a 2 or 4 p.m. (1400 or 1600) burn to capture the most active time of day for fire. We adjusted *Foliar moisture content* from 120 % at our low end 80th % ERC to 80 % at the high end 99th percentile ERC. Whatever time of day you choose for your analysis, the total length of the fuel conditioning period should be at least seven days (**Figure 7**).

Users may also want to consider generating additional CFR maps for each fire behavior threshold by varying the input parameters (uphill as well as directional winds, for instance). Combining all output files for a given weather threshold will create a probability map.

Repeat this step for every subunit in your analysis area.

TASKS
1. Load the FARSITE **landscape file (.lcp) into** FLAMMAP.

2. Choose *Analysis Area - New Run – Inputs*

    2.1 Load fuel moisture (<%>.fms) files, weather(<%>.wtr), and wind (<%>.wnd) for the relevant threshold condition.

    2.2 Set *Winds Blowing* Uphill.

    2.3 Set *Wind Speed (*20' windspeed) for the particular percentile class.

OR set *Wind Direction and Azimuth* if specifying wind direction other than uphill.

3. **Establish fuel conditioning period.**

4. **Establish time of burn.** Setting the *Fuel Moisture Conditioning Period, End Day, Time* according to times set in your .wtr and .wnd files.

5. **Choose** *Outputs* **and check appropriate output grid boxes. Run the simulation.**

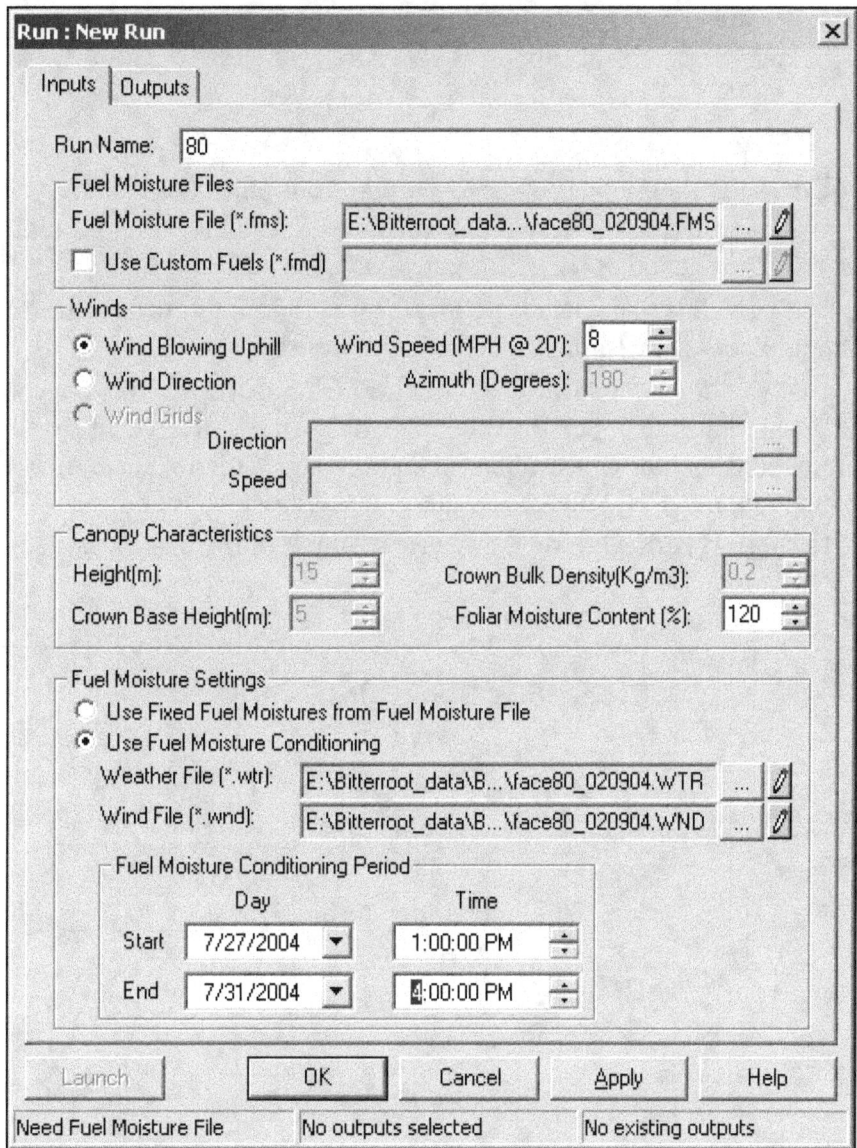

Figure 7 - Run FlamMap.

6. **Export the outputs.** Right click on *Run Name*, right click on the appropriate output grid, S*ave as* .asc file. If running ROS, be sure to export with 2 decimal places and in m/min.

7. Import the .asc grids into GIS, merge together, and re-project to match resource base data (if necessary).

Step 4. Creating a fire effects library _____

ACTION: Use the fire effects crosswalk to link fire behavior to fire effects.

DISCUSSION: This step will result in a number of fire effects maps which can be printed out and/or saved on a CD and made available to management units and included in fire data packages for incident support (**Figure 8**).

TASKS
1. Merge the FLAMMAP **output grid to your baseline GIS data** (vegetation, soils and/or aquatics), preserving all attributes of each layer. (This requires that your baseline data be in GRID format.)
   1.1. Add new field, calculate the concatenated field for your baseline data (see Mapping Ecosystem Targets, discussed previously).
2. Link fire effects crosswalk to merged GIS data. Use the concatenated field as the 'join' item. Sort and check to make sure you have all possible combinations in your crosswalk (if you find blanks, then you are missing those combinations). Adjust your crosswalk as necessary (see Figure 4).
3. Create fire effects library. Save each output of fire effects as a separate GIS layer.

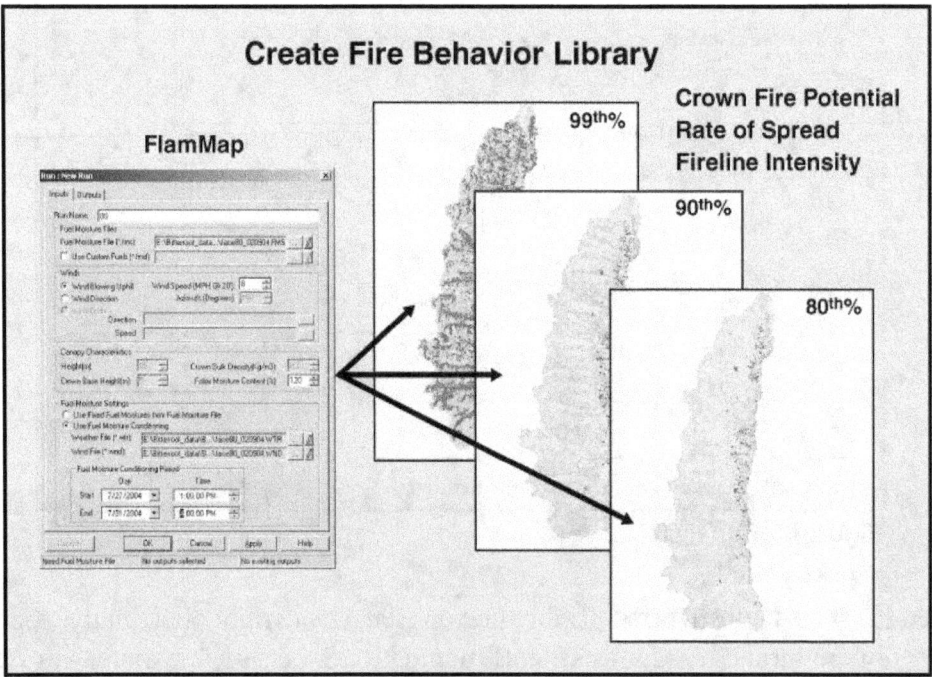

Figure 8 - Fire Effects Library using FlamMap.

B

Current Conditions Using a Landscape-level, Stochastic Model

In this section we illustrate how a stochastic, landscape dynamics simulator program can be used to identify current fire behavior and likely effects on key resources (**Figure 9**). The goal is to identify probabilities of fire and probable fire type under a variety of weather and climatic conditions. We use SIMPPLLE a landscape-level, stochastic model that predicts and tracks vegetative succession and disturbances (fire, insects, disease, management) at a landscape scale. SIMPPLLE's rule-based architecture allows users to adjust many successional and disturbance parameters (type of fire, likelihood of wind driven event, and so forth). Before running a simulation, users should always evaluate the default values and inquire about revised files for their area.

We used SIMPPLLE Version 2.2 (based on irregular polygons) and 2.3 (in its 'pseudo-grid', or regular polygon, mode) and conducted analysis in both ArcView 3.2 (with Spatial Analyst) and ArcGIS 8.1.

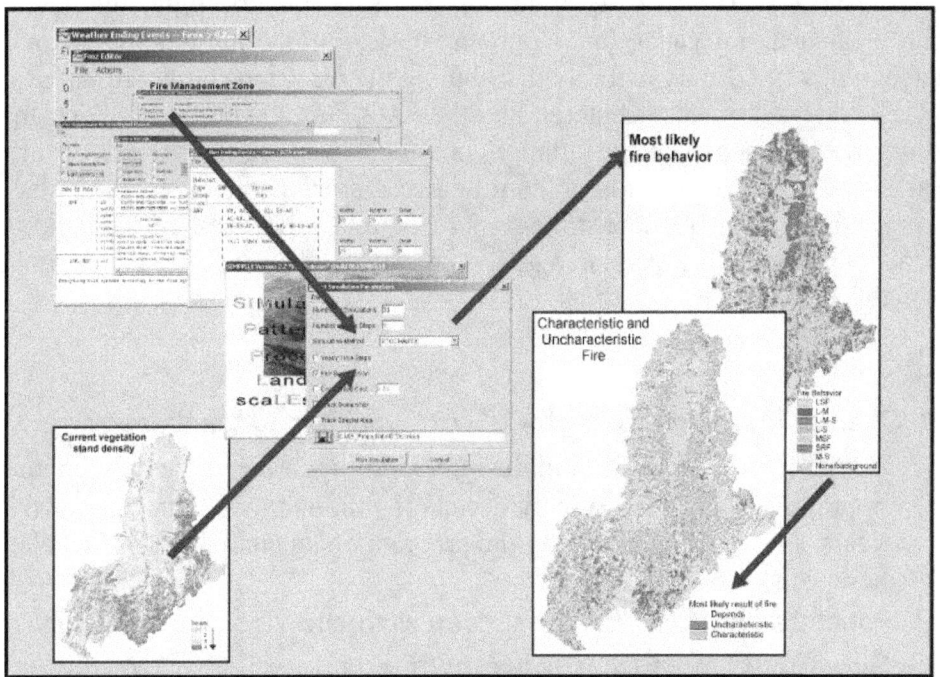

Figure 9- Overview of B current conditions using a landscape-level, stochastic model.

Step 1. Parameterizing the model

ACTION: Evaluate and update, if necessary, SIMPPLLE parameter defaults.

DISCUSSION: SIMPPLLE uses vector coverages to distribute ecological processes (fire and treatments) and track changes within and across simulations. While it refers to these as ownership, Fire Management Zone (FMZ), and an optional Special Area, these can actually refer to any geographic subdivision or reporting unit the user decides. Please refer to the SIMPPLLE user's guide for instructions on how to change attribute fields and create SIMPPLLE coverages.

SIMPPLLE uses graphical interface screens to assist users in editing the various logic screens. Because these screens can only be viewed separately, we have created an Excel spreadsheet to capture the logic comprehensively. Initially, these must be filled out manually, but once created, they provide a quick easy-reference for defaults, as well as reviewing and tracking changes. All defaults for the Bitterroot National Forest (11/2003) are shown comprehensively in run_template.xls (see Forms and CD at end of document).

1.1 Create an historical fire start cover

DISCUSSION: SIMPPLLE distributes fire starts by converting the number of starts per FMZ (annual or decadal) into a per-acre basis, multiplying this by the total acreage in that FMZ and randomly distributing the resulting starts within the assigned FMZ. Historical start data is entered into the *FMZ Editor*. The fire size designations on this screen assist in a cost estimation, not in determining fire growth or ultimate fire size. Users may also choose to confine fire and/or treatments to particular areas (by ownership or management strategy, for example, wilderness or wildland-urban interface) by eliminating starts in a geographic area. Historical fire data may be obtained from KCFAST on the web.

TASKS

1. **Overlay historical fire starts with your Fire Management Zones/Units (FMZ).** Sum the number of lightning starts (human, too, if appropriate) by FMZ. Sum by decade if your SIMPPLLE time step will be 10 years; sum by year if running the program on an annual basis. Calculate the acreage of each FMZ.

2. **Populate the *FMZ Editor* screen with the fire start information.** Select *System Knowledge → Vegetative Process →Fire Occurrence Input* and enter your fire start information by Fire Management Zone (**Figure 10**).

3. **Save file and track file name** for future reference (see the fire occurrence workshop in run_template.xls at the end of this document for an example).

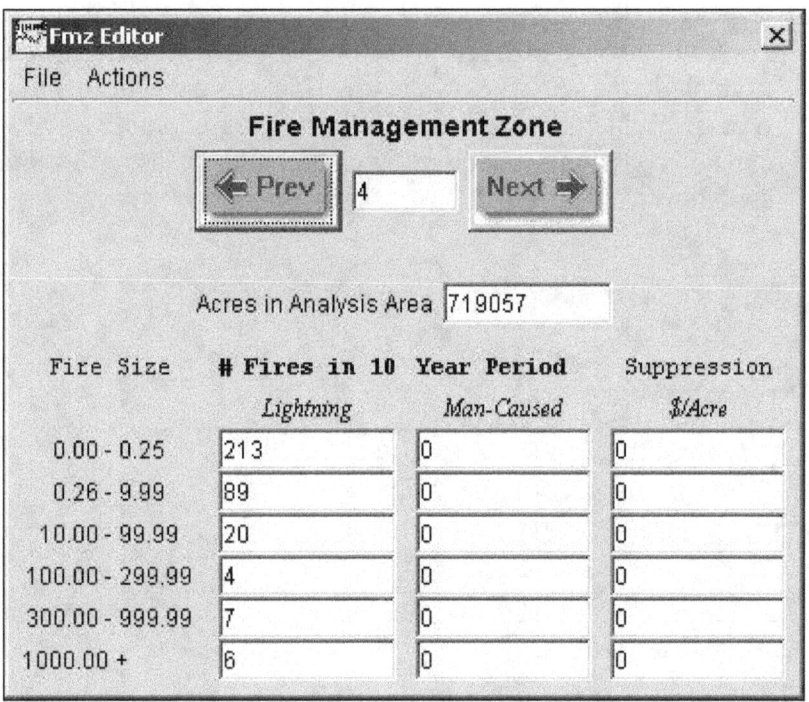

Figure 10 - SIMPPLLE's *Fire Occurrence Input* for entering fire history.

1.2 Set fire management and fire weather logic

DISCUSSION: SIMPPLLE offers users a number of opportunities to adjust both fire suppression effort and efficiency rates. Specific file names (and the manner in which the file affects fire management) include:

- Fire suppression for Class A fires (effort and efficiency),
- Fire suppression for beyond Class A (effort),
- Weather ending events for fires < 0.25 acres (efficiency),
- Weather ending events for fires > 0.25 acres (probability),
- Extreme fire probability (probability), and
- Regional climate (weather)

To identify the consequences of changing or establishing a Wildland Fire Use (WFU) zone, these are the files you need to adjust (see SIMPPLLE user's guide to check field type).

The qualitative weather settings, which cannot be adjusted by the user, are based on weather and climate conditions over the past 50 years – generally the time period over which our knowledge of ecosystem processes has been developed.

TASKS

1. **Evaluate and adjust** *Fire Suppression for Class A fires* **data, as necessary.** This screen allows one to model various suppression efficiency rates, or to consider the effect of not suppressing any Wilderness fires. To do so, set efficiency to 0 for Wilderness.

1.1. Choose *System Knowledge→Vegetative Process→Fire Suppression Logic→ Class A* (**Figure 11**). Settings are read as efficiency levels. For example in the screen shown below, 75 % of the class A fires in non-forest types in Wilderness are successfully suppressed under Normal and Wetter climatic conditions, but none are caught at the Class A level under Drier conditions.

(a) Class A fires.

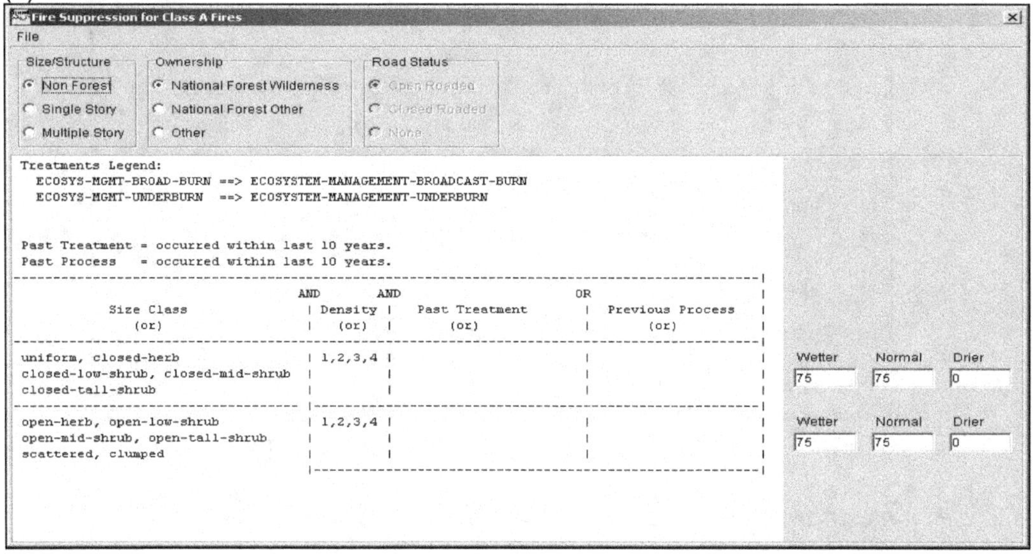

(b) Beyond class A.

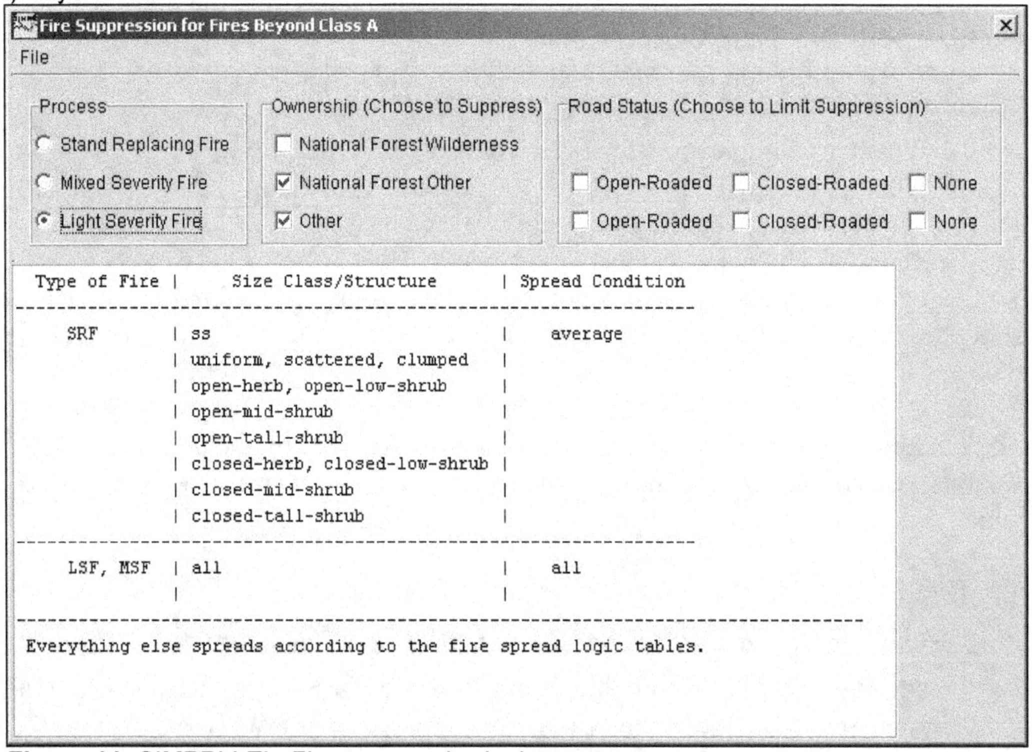

Figure 11- SIMPPLLE's *Fire suppression* logic screens.

2. Evaluate and adjust *Fire Suppression Beyond Class A* data as necessary.
This file offers another place to limit fire suppression. If you choose to apply a no suppression tactic in roadless and Wilderness areas, check the appropriate boxes under Road Status, and uncheck appropriate boxes under Ownership.

    2.1. Choose *System Knowledge→Vegetative Process→Fire Suppression Logic→Beyond Class A.*

3. Evaluate and adjust *Weather Ending Events ---Fires < 0.25* data, as necessary. This screen allows the user to adjust fire ending events for the normal climatic condition and to model changes due to climate shifts (**Figure 12**).

    3.1. Choose *System Knowledge→Vegetative Process→Weather Ending Events→ Fires Less than .25 Acres.* Settings are read as probability of fire events ending fire under various climatic conditions. In Figure 12 (a), 25 % of fires under ¼ acre in Engelmann spruce are put out by weather under normal climatic conditions; 50 % under wetter conditions, and none under drier conditions. These probabilities can be altered by the user. In order to change the habitat types or species for which these apply, one must work with the SIMPPLLE team to change hard-wired inputs.

4. Evaluate and adjust *Weather Ending Events ---Fires > 0.25* data, as necessary. Settings in this file adjust the probability that a weather event will extinguish fires of various sizes greater than ¼ acre.

    4.1. Choose *System Knowledge→Vegetative Process→Weather Ending Events→ Fires greater than .25 Acres.* File is read as probability. In the example shown in Figure 12 (b), there is no possibility that fires less than 500 acres and a 75 % probability that a fire of greater than 50,000 acres will eventually be put out by a weather event.

(a) Fires < 0.25 acres.

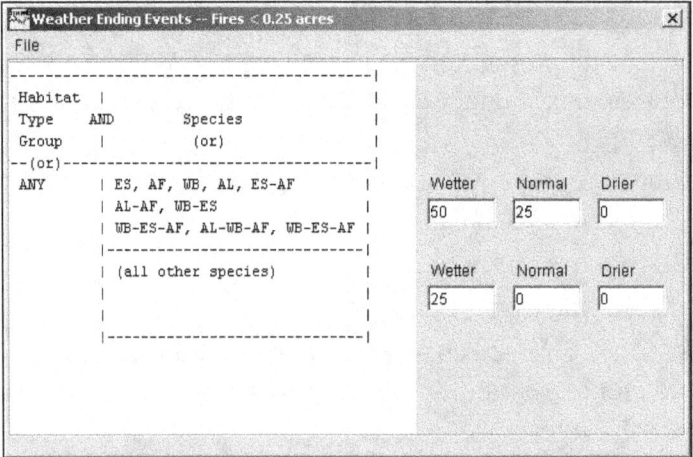

(b) Fires > 0.25 acres.

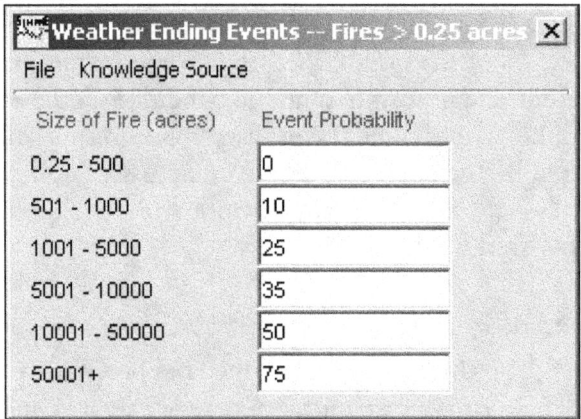

Figure 12- SIMPPLLE's Weather ending event screens.

5. **Evaluate and adjust** *Extreme Fire Spread Probability* **data, as necessary.** This file allows the user to control the dry, windy conditions under which a fire may escape or become large.

5.1. Choose *System Knowledge→Vegetative Process→Extreme Fire Spread Probability.* The *Probability due to weather event* is the probability that weather drives the fire while *Fire event acres for 100 percent probability* sets the fire acreage at which the incident may begin to drive internal weather condition. These settings should be based upon knowledge of frequency of weather-driven extreme fire behavior and local conditions. For example, setting *probability due to weather event* at 100 % and *Fire event acres for 100 percent probability* at 0 will force all fires to act with extreme behavior. Alternatively, setting the *probability due to weather event* at 100 %, but specifying a much larger acreage, say 10,000 acres for *Fire event acres for 100 percent probability* specifies that only fires greater than 10,000 acres will exhibit extreme behavior due to plume-domination.

6. Use the *Regional Climate* file to adjust for wet/dry cycles. This file allows the user to determine the climatic regime for each step in a SIMPPLLE run. Choices are wetter, normal, and drier. Default is normal. Variations in annual moisture, such as to model drought cycles (wetter, drier, and normal) are first specified in the *Regional climate* file. *Fire suppression for Class A fires, Weather ending events for fires < 0.25 acres* and *Type of Fire Logic* tables can then all be adjusted to reflect different responses to different regional climatic conditions.

> **6.1.** Choose *System Knowledge→Regional Climate.*

1.3 Set fire behavior logic

DISCUSSION: SIMPPLLE offers users the ability to specify and adjust fire spread. Fire spread is discussed in terms of fire type (light, mixed, or stand-replacing fire). Fire spread is influenced by the relative position (adjacency) and type of fire in a neighboring polygon, as well as the receiving stand's density, size structure, and past processes (fire, insects, disease, treatments, and so forth). The user may specify the type of fire in the receiving stand under average or extreme weather conditions. Values for fire spread are stored in files with the following extensions: firespread and fire logic (**Figure 13**).

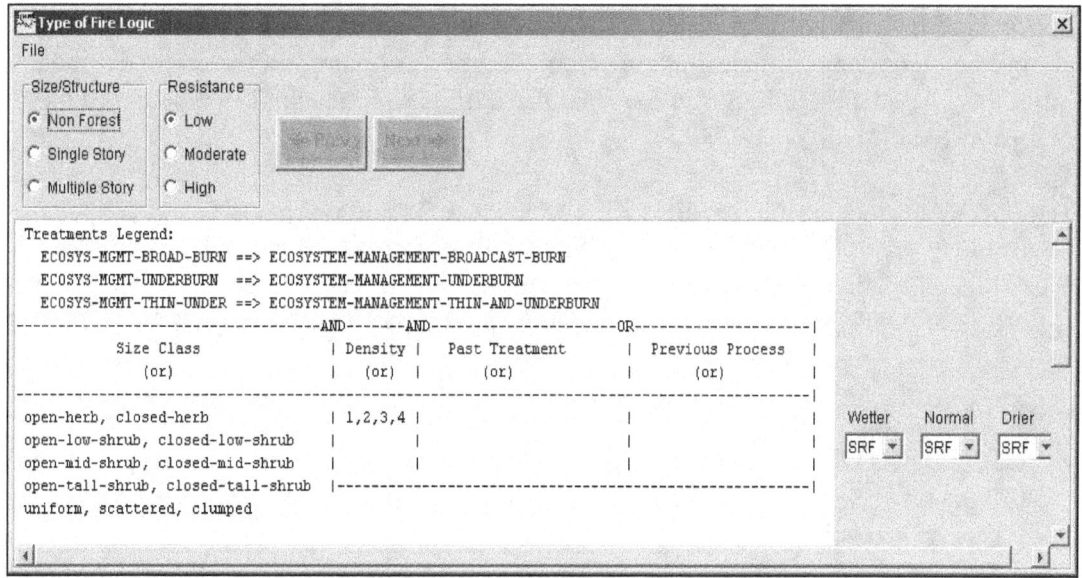

Figure 13- SIMPPLLE's *Type of fire logic* screen.

TASKS

> **1. Evaluate fire spread logic.** Choose *System Knowledge→Vegetative Process→Fire Spread Logic.* Make adjustments as needed. *Save* file.
>
> > **1.1** Populate run_template.xls.fire spread logic to facilitate review and to track changes.

2. Evaluate Type of Fire Logic. Choose *System Knowledge→Vegetative Process→Type of Fire Logic*. Make adjustments as needed. *Save* file.

    2.1 Populate run_template.xls.type of fire logic to facilitate review and to track changes.

Step 2. Creating fire type and probability maps _____

ACTION: Run 30 iterations of SIMPPLLE (decadal time step) for historic and current conditions and generate probability maps.

DISCUSSION: SIMPPLLE developers recommend running 30 iterations of each simulation to capture the full range of ecosystem process variability. Output files (.txt) provide the probability that any given stand (polygon) will burn with a particular severity. This information is used to create maps of most probable fire type, probability of burning, probable fire frequency (on a per pixel or polygon-basis), and probable fire return interval or departure from historic fire regime map. Which type of summary you choose depends on what you are trying to determine and whether you want to work with probabilities of conditions or actual conditions.

Once run, users must choose between evaluating a single iteration (which will provide a single version) or evaluating the total probability summed across all iterations. One option is to graph a vegetation attribute such as Species across all simulations, then choose a single iteration that illustrates the conditions you are interested in: average, high, low. Another is to translate the final probabilities into a single value based on highest probability.

SIMPPLLE creates multiple .txt files for every iteration; some are quite large. It is advisable to create a new directory for each analysis and save the runs to this folder. After the simulation is complete, save the probability, spread, update, and GIS files. Refer to the SIMPPLLE user's manual for additional background and instructions.

2.1 Create an historic fire regime map

DISCUSSION: To create an historical coverage, unburnable cover types such as urban and agriculture - as well as any cover types and pathways that incorporate introduced species - must be set to a probable historical class and/or pathway.

TASKS
1. **Reclassify urban and agriculture cover types (Species) to an historic cover type.** Reset, or reclass, any introduced/exotic/weed cover types and pathways to historical conditions.
2. **Run 30 iterations of a 50 decade simulation (decadal time steps),** specifying historic pathways and no fire suppression. Save in a new folder.

3. **Load the .area file for last decade of last simulation** and run 30 iterations of a single decade using historic pathways and no fire suppression. Save to a subfolder of historic folder.

4. **Determine probability of burn and most probable fire type (Figure 14).**

  4.1. In a database manager open the *-n-process.txt* file for the single decade simulation. Strip and save the SLINK and fire attribute fields in a new .txt file. NOTE: EXCEL will only accept 65,000+ records. It truncates larger files, but will perform analyses. Use another program (Arc, or SPSS) to work with large files.

  4.2. Add a field and sum probabilities for Light, Mixed and Stand Replacing fire. This is the probability of fire.

  4.3. Add another field and calculate the maximum of Light, Mixed, and Stand Replacing fire. This is the most probable fire type.

  4.4. Save file as .txt or .dbf and link table to coverage using Stand-Id field in GIS. Sum acres, sort by Special Area and sum acres, map, and so forth.

5. **Link the new .txt file to the GIS coverage to create probability maps.** Add the .txt file to your Arc project and join to the base vegetation coverage using the SLINK as the join field.

2.2. Create a current conditions map

TASKS

1. **Determine probability of burn and most probable fire type**

  1.1 In a database manager open the *-n-process.txt* file for the simulation. Strip and save SLINK and fire fields in a new .txt file. NOTE: EXCEL will only accept 65,000+ records. It truncates larger files, but will perform analyses. Use another program – ARC, or SPSS – to work with large files.

  1.2. Add a field and sum probabilities for Light, Mixed and Stand Replacing fire. This is the total probability of fire field.

  1.3 Add an additional field and calculate the maximum of Light, Mixed and Stand Replacing fire. This is the most likely fire type (or probable burn type) field.

  1.4 Save file as .txt or .dbf.

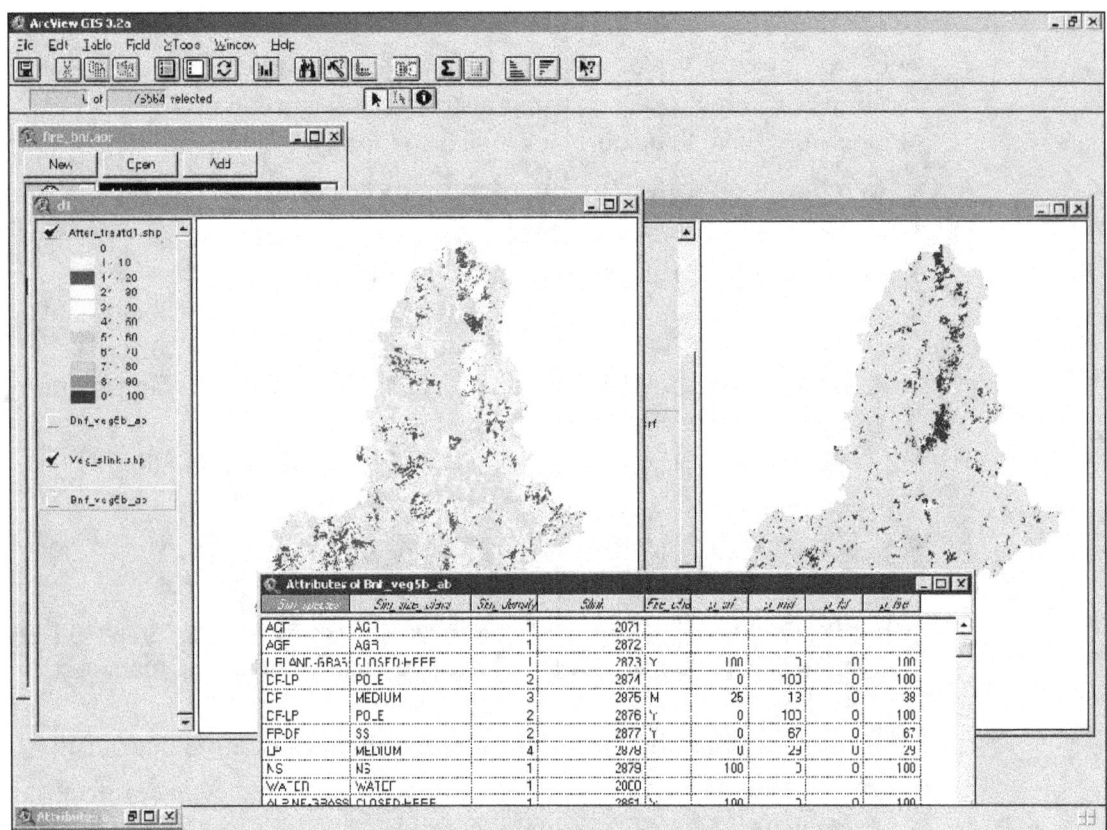

Figure 14- Calculating probable fire type in SIMPPLLE.

Step 3. Creating fire effects maps _____

ACTION: Apply fire effects cross-walk to map probabilities.

TASKS
1. Add the .txt or .dbf created above and use the SLINK field to join the table to the vegetation coverage.
2. Create separate GIS layers for the various probability maps you would like. Post these on an intranet website and add information about these maps to data provided to incident support teams.

C

Future Conditions Using a Stand-based, Deterministic Model

Predicting future fire behavior using a stand-based, deterministic model requires development of fuels data for some future vegetative condition (**Figure 15**). To accomplish this task, three decisions must be made:

- What base data and software will be used to create and compare current and future fire behavior predictions?
- How will future vegetation attributes be assigned to probability data?
- What algorithm will be used to create fuels data from vegetation attributes?

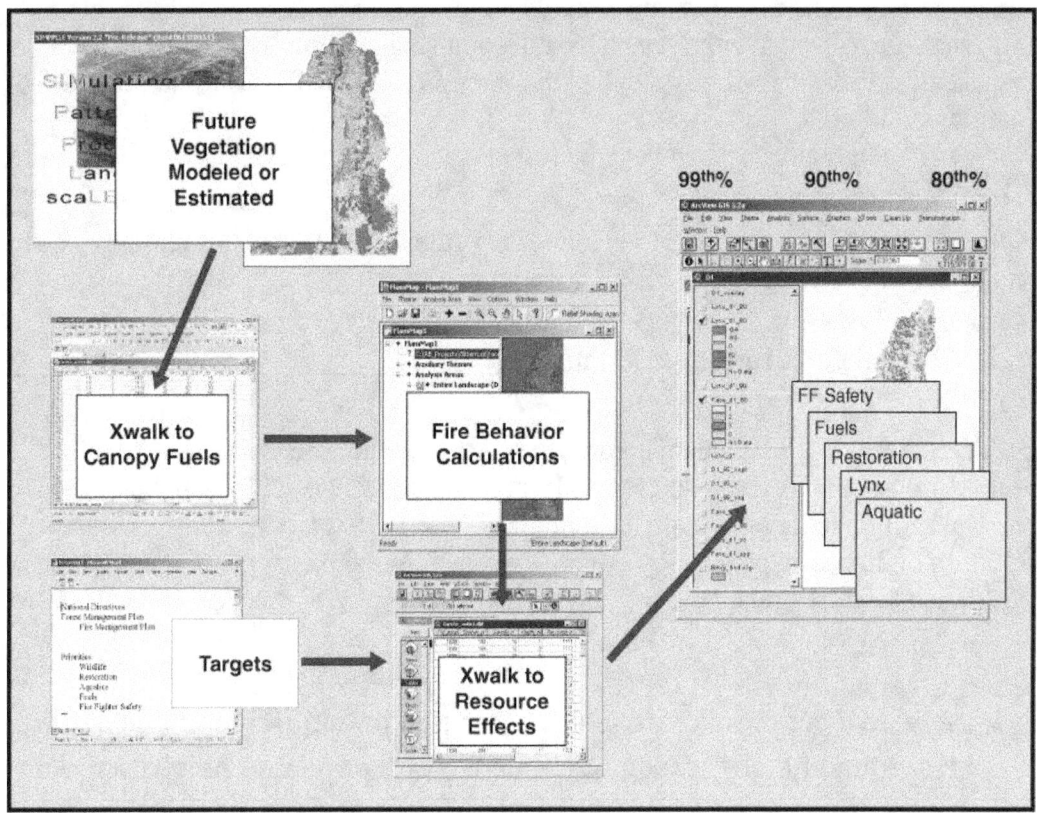

Figure 15 - Overview of *C* future conditions using a stand-based, deterministic model.

Step 1. Creating a future vegetation map _____

DISCUSSION: One can develop a map of future vegetation conditions by either selectively changing the fuels condition of specific areas, or creating a entirely new vegetation map using an LSDM. A key consideration, though, is that if your goal is to compare the existing condition to a potential future, then use the same base data source *and* the same algorithm to specify fuels from vegetative conditions.

In our work on the Bitterroot National Forest, we used SIMPPLLE to generate the future vegetative conditions. However, comparing a FLAMMAP run based on fuels derived from a 2002/2003 satellite image to a prediction of future vegetation based on significantly different vegetation data would not yield the necessary 'apples to apples' comparison. Thus, we used SIMPPLLE to generate both the current and future vegetation coverages.

Since SIMPPLLE is a stochastic model, summary data for a multi-iteration simulation are expressed as probabilities. To obtain a single condition for each key attribute (cover type, density, structure) one can either use output from a single iteration (representing the mean or an extreme condition) or translate the summary probability files into most likely vegetation condition.

TASKS

See next section (D) for directions to create a future vegetation simulation using SIMPPLLE.

Step 2. Creating a future fuels map _____

DISCUSSION: We adapted an algorithm created by the Fire Behavior Modeling Institute (Fire Lab) to develop 2003 FARSITE fuels data for use with SIMPPLLE, then used this new algorithm to develop both current and future FARSITE data. This crosswalk uses information on habitat type, canopy cover, size class, and cover type to generate the five FARSITE fuels grids (**Figure 16**).

TASKS

1. Develop a crosswalk between vegetation attributes and FARSITE fuels data (stand height, canopy bulk density, crown base height, crown closure, fuel model).

   1.1. Create a .dbf (or .txt) identifying the five FARSITE fuels values for each unique combination of vegetation cover type, structure, and density variables. Use the same 'primary ecosystem component' variable discussed in Chapter 1. Join this new table to the GIS cover of future vegetation and create separate grids of each FARSITE fuels field.

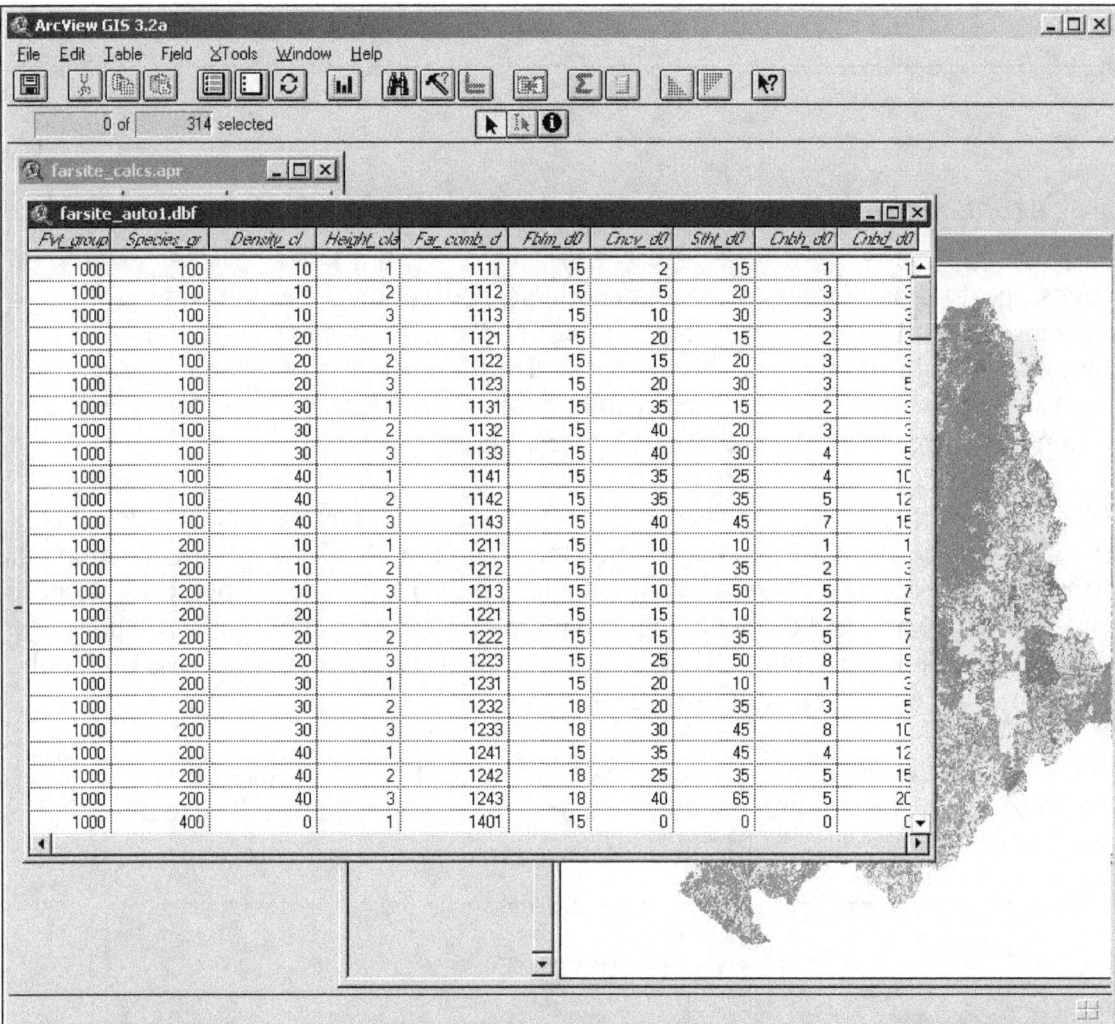

Figure 16 - Illustration of the crosswalk between future vegetative conditions and FARSITE fuel layers.

Step 3. Identifying change_____ _____

ACTION: Use the fire behavior-fire effects crosswalks to identify changes.

DISCUSSION: Although the results of such an analysis may have questionable cell to ground validity (depending upon the degree of ground-truthing), the process does yield an 'apples to apples' comparison useful for strategic fire planning. For instance, this type of analysis can identify whether future conditions as a result of particular management strategies are likely to be generally 'better' or 'worse' than the current situation.

TASKS

Follow the steps outlined in Section **A** Step **4**, above.

D

Future Conditions Using a Stochastic, Landscape-level Model

Landscape dynamics models offer the opportunity for 'gaming': the comparison of outcomes under different management strategies. Being stochastic in nature, it is necessary to run multiple iterations to capture the full range of ecosystem variability. If the real range of variability has been captured, the actual future should fall somewhere within this range of variation described by the multiple iterations.

To use a stochastic landscape dynamics model for planning, you must make a decision about how to view and use simulation outcomes. You can identify a specific iteration (an average or an extreme) to choose or use the final probabilities. For our purposes, we need to be able to identify and extract a single condition for each vegetation attribute at each target time period. Thus, the choice is between using a single iteration and translating the final probabilities into the most likely condition.

In this section we describe how to use SIMPPLLE to identify stands for treatment, enter these into SIMPPLLE as either specific units or random units, and re-calculate fire effects (**Figure 17**).

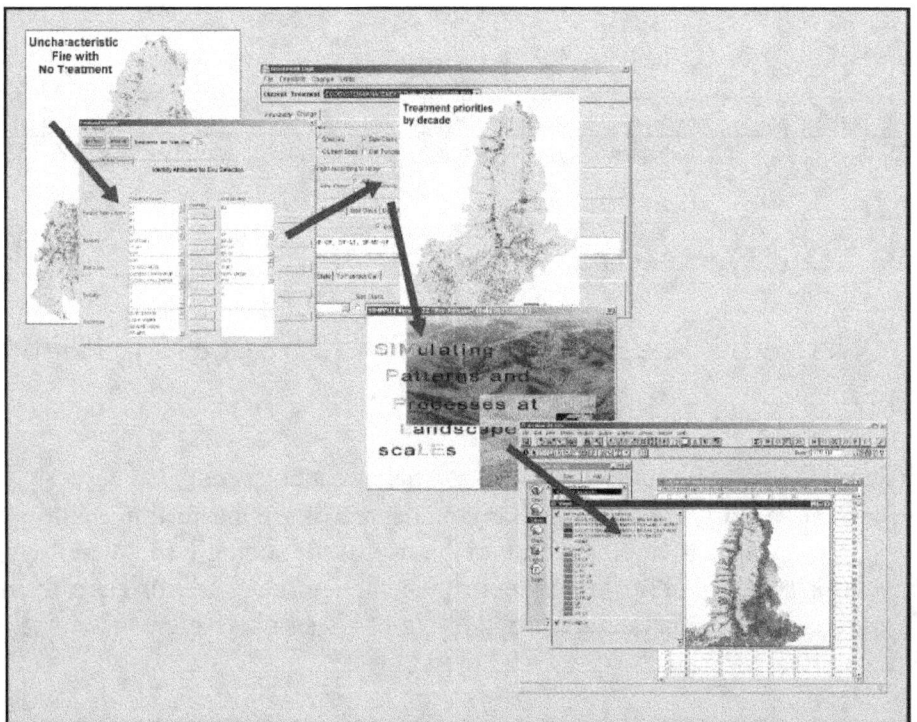

Figure 17 - Overview of D future conditions using a landscape-level, stochastic model.

Step 1. Identifying and prioritizing stands

DISCUSSION: Data used to address prioritization are the output from the effects determination (see Section A Step 4 or Section B Step 3, above). Treatment options vary by fire effects. Where fire is likely to result in characteristic effects under low to normal weather conditions, prescribed fire or even Wildland Fire Use may be an option. Mechanical treatment is necessary prior to reintroduction of fire in areas where fire effects are likely to be uncharacteristic under any weather conditions.

There are several approaches to prioritization. In this example, we prioritize stands based on a comparison between likely within-stand effects of fire and desired stand conditions. It is possible to use this concept to consider ecological effects within a landscape context. Since SIMPPLLE does not at this time model the physical process of fire, it does not provide information on rate of spread or other quantitative fire behavior parameters. Thus, if the goal is to identify stands that are the greatest contributors to spread of fire across the landscape, another program such as those based on the FARSITE /FLAMMAP family (Finney, in development) should be used.

Here, we prioritize stands based on effects that are likely to be undesirable. In a planning process, this would be integrated with other criteria and a final set of stands identified. We then use a simulation model to test the results of treating stands identified and determining the future conditions – fire behavior, cost, and so forth.

SIDEBAR 2: Identifying priority treatment areas
We used three criteria to identify priority treatment areas.

    (1) First, we determined and mapped 'at risk' stands. Primary cover types of concern are ponderosa pine (*Pinus ponderosa*), Douglas-fir (*Pseudotsuga menziesii*) and western larch (*Larix occidentalis*). Uncharacteristic fire types in these cover types we defined as crown fire in stands with larger diameter trees. For this example we used SIMPPLLE to identify 'at risk' stands, but one could use FLAMMAP as well.

    (2) Next, we buffered the Bitterroot National Forest's urban interface fire management zone by one mile and selected 'at risk' stands within this zone.

    (3) Finally, we identified areas of high erosion hazard within watersheds currently containing westslope cutthroat trout, a critical wildlife species on the Forest.
    Our illustrations show the convergence of high crown fire danger and WUI in one map (Figure 18a), and high crown fire danger and wildlife in another (Figure 18b).

    Most likely, you will apply several criteria then use a weighting or ranking system to combine the criteria maps to arrive at a final solution.

(a) At risk stands within 1 mile of the WUI.

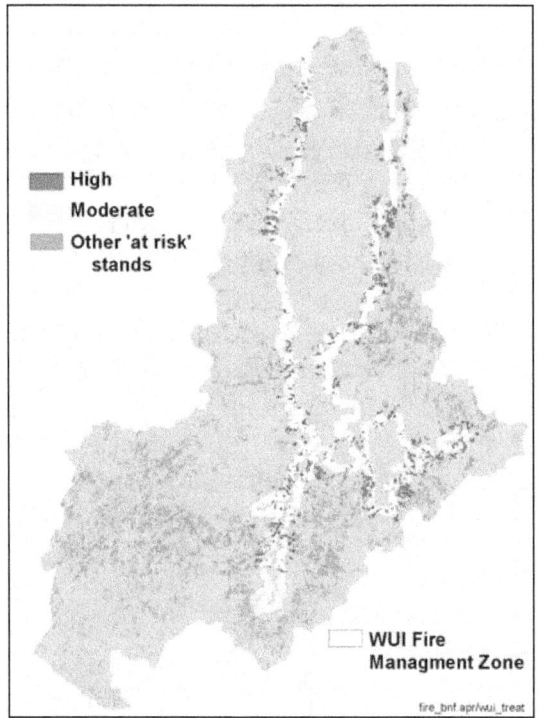

(b) Areas of high erosion potential in critical watersheds.

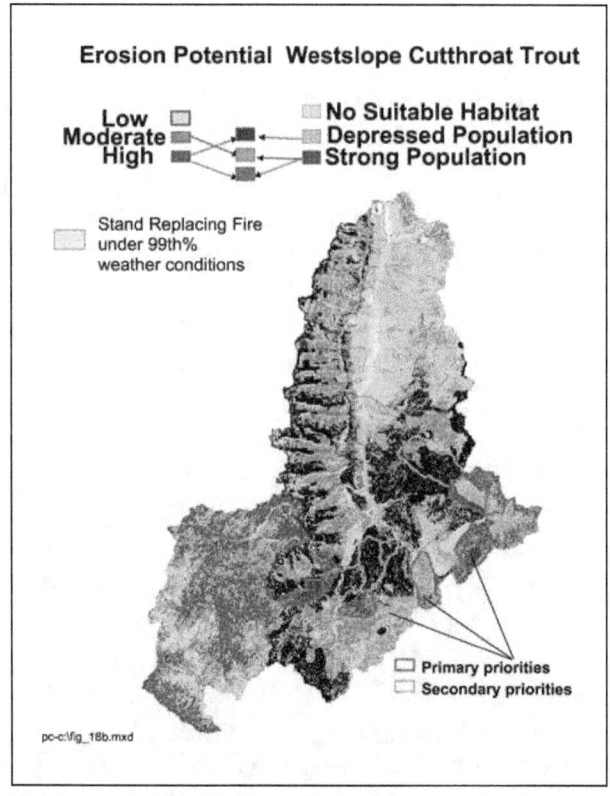

Figure 18 - Potential treatment priorities identified by proximity to the wildland-urban interface, stands 'at risk' of uncharacteristic fire, and sensitive wildlife habitat.

Step 2. Creating treatment schedules _____

DISCUSSION: Scheduling fuels activities can be accomplished in SIMPPLLE by either identifying the specific stands to treat (Option 1), or allowing the program to randomly select stands meeting certain criteria (Option 2). There are a number of ways to identify stands to treat. One is to use either FLAMMAP or SIMPPLLE to identify highest priority locations by spatial location or stand criteria. Note that random treatments will change within-stand conditions, but may or may not affect landscape-scale processes such as species movement, migration, or fire movement.

We began by identifying stand structure conditions meeting our cover type criteria (dense, multi-story stands), then selecting and exporting these records from our GIS vegetation cover. We used this list to create an input file for SIMPPLLE.

Option 1: Identifying specific treatment units
TASKS

1. **Generate a .txt file of stand-id's to be treated**, by decade (by year if running SIMPPLLE in annual mode). Stand-id's must be those used in the SIMPPLLE coverage. Specific stands may be identified using any number of criteria. One way is to use the stands identified in previous analysis (either FLAMMAP or SIMPPLLE) in which fire poses a 'risk'.

    1.1. In Arc, *export* the .dbf associated with selected stands to EXCEL.

    1.2. Eliminate all fields except for the stand-id.

    1.3. *Save as* .txt file.

    1.4. In a text editor, open and add treatment name on the first line of the file exactly as shown in SIMPPLLE's *System Knowledge→ Vegetative Treatments→ Treatment Logic→Current Treatment* screen.

2. **Load the .txt file** into SIMPPLLE. In SIMPPLLE, open *System Knowledge→ Vegetative Treatment→ Treatment Schedule→ Load Unit Id File.*

3. **Determine upper acreage limit** for each simulation step (decade or year) and enter in *Treatment Schedule.* Track files in run_template.xls.

4. **Evaluate, and adjust if necessary, default treatment effects.** These determine stand condition following treatment.

    4.1. Open *System Knowledge→ Vegetative Treatments→ Treatment Logic* (**Figure 19**).

    4.2. Choose a *Current Treatment* and activate one of the vegetation classes listed under *Feasibility.*

    4.3. Choose *Change* and evaluate the logic. It is helpful to view *Pseudo-Code Text* to help understand how to read the screen.

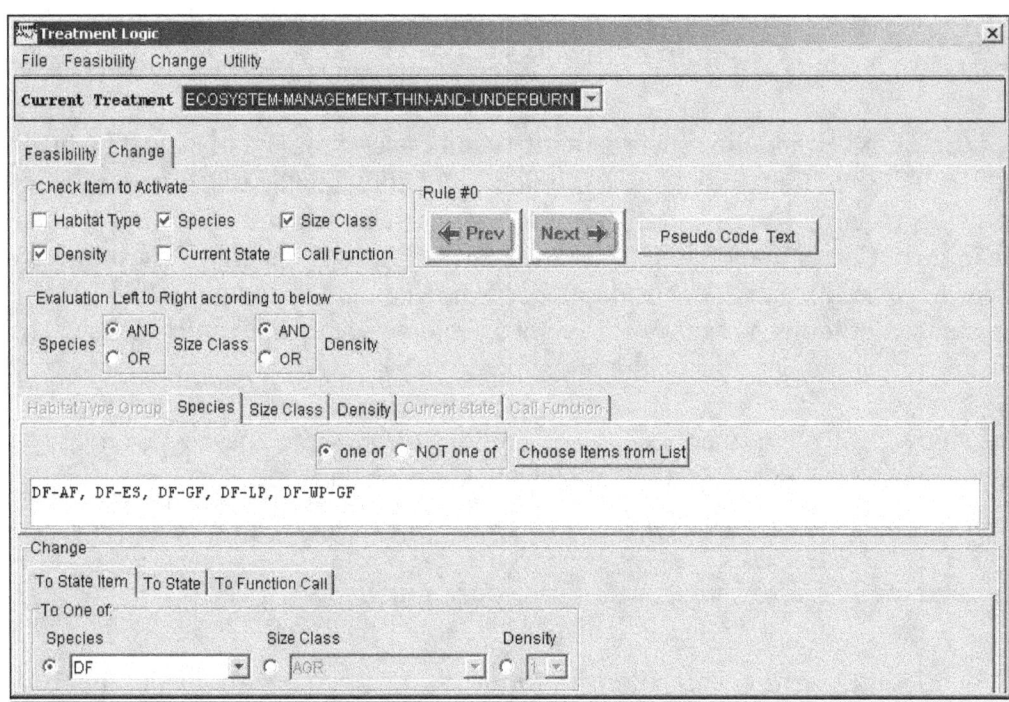

Figure 19 - SIMPPLLE's *Treatment Logic* screen.

Option 2: Randomly selecting treatment units
TASKS

1. Identify the stand conditions for treatment. Conditions may include habitat type, species, size class, and density. The *Treatment Scheduler* is used to identify stand types for treatment. *Treatment Logic* is used to determine the effects of treatment.

    1.1. Open *System Knowledge→ Vegetative Treatment→ Treatment Schedule* (**Figure 20**). Choose *File→ New Treatment*. Choose from among the possible choices for each time step.

    1.2. Identify the *Desired acres* to treat in each time step.

    1.3. If applicable, select *Special Area* and/or *Road Status*. This will be necessary if one does not want to treat roadless, wilderness, or private lands, or alternatively, if one wishes to confine treatments to a particular type of area, such as the Wildland-Urban Interface.

    1.4. Evaluate, and adjust if necessary, defaults in *Treatment Logic*.

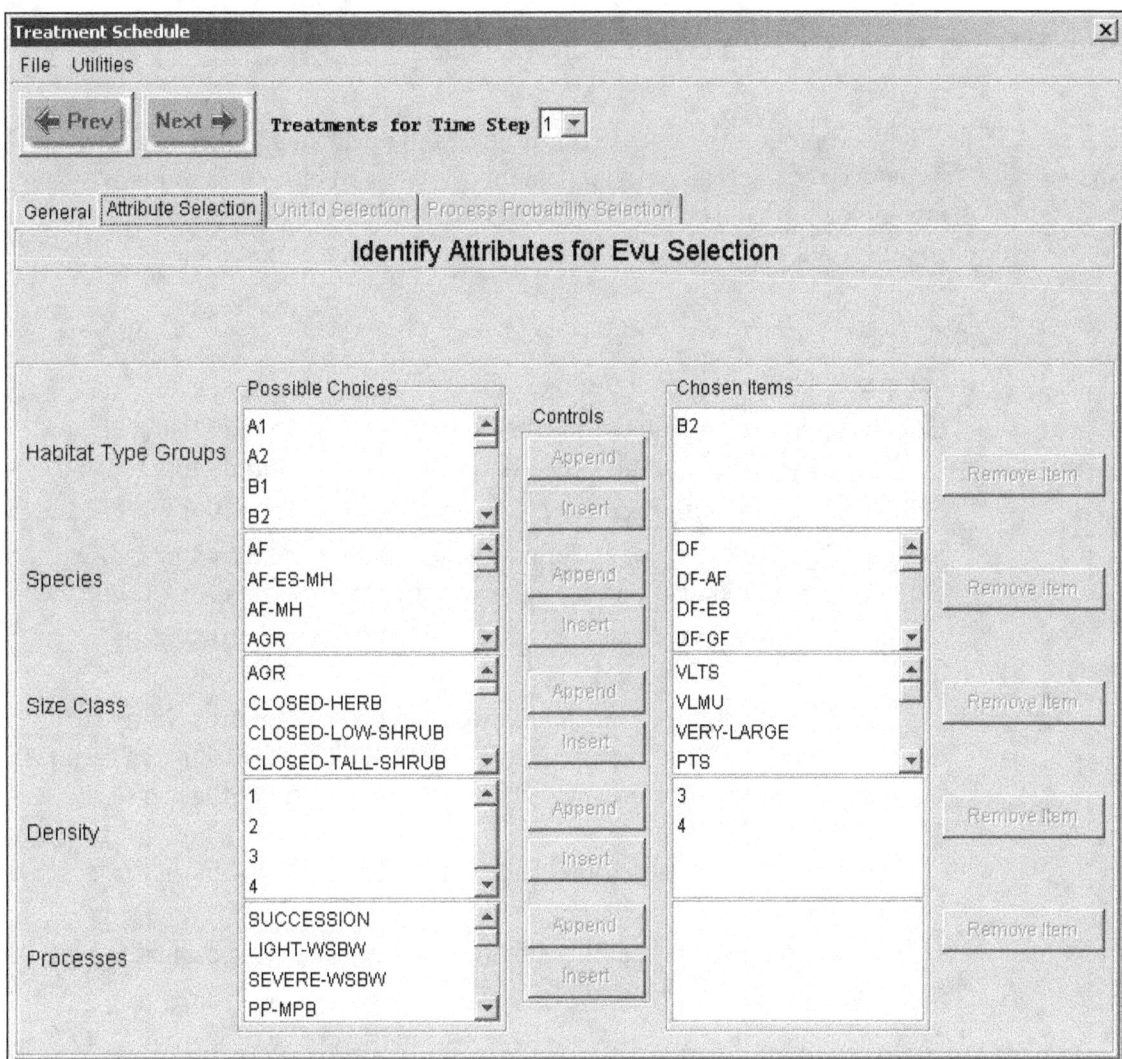

Figure 20 - SIMPPLLE's *Treatment Scheduler* screen.

Step 3. Creating fire type and probability maps _____

TASKS

Follow directions under Section **B** Step **2**, above, to create fire type and probability maps.

Step 4. Comparing fire type and probability maps _____

DISCUSSION: Completing these tasks allows users to perform an effects analysis by analyzing consequences of alternative management scenarios. This is one of many ways to conduct change detection. We conducted the same analysis using grids and vectors. Here we describe the vector steps; these can be conducted at the same time.

TASKS
1. Compare fire probabilities.

1.1. Join the fire portions of the *–n-process.txt* files to the SIMPPLLE coverage (or use SIMPPLLE's ArcView extension to do this for you).

1.1.a Edit the *–n-process.txt* files to eliminate all but the fire fields. Rename the fields to reflect the appropriate simulation. **1.2.** Add two new fields, one for each simulation.

1.2.a. Sum *Light, Mixed,* and *Stand Replacing* fire probabilities for each simulation.

1.2.b. Add another new field and subtract one total probability from the other (for example, subtracting historic from current results in negatives for decreases and positive number for increases in probability).

1.2.c. Save as .txt file, load back into ARCVIEW, and join to SIMPPLLE coverage.

1.3. Map change in probability of fire severity class. It is easiest to hide fields not in use (**Figure 21**).

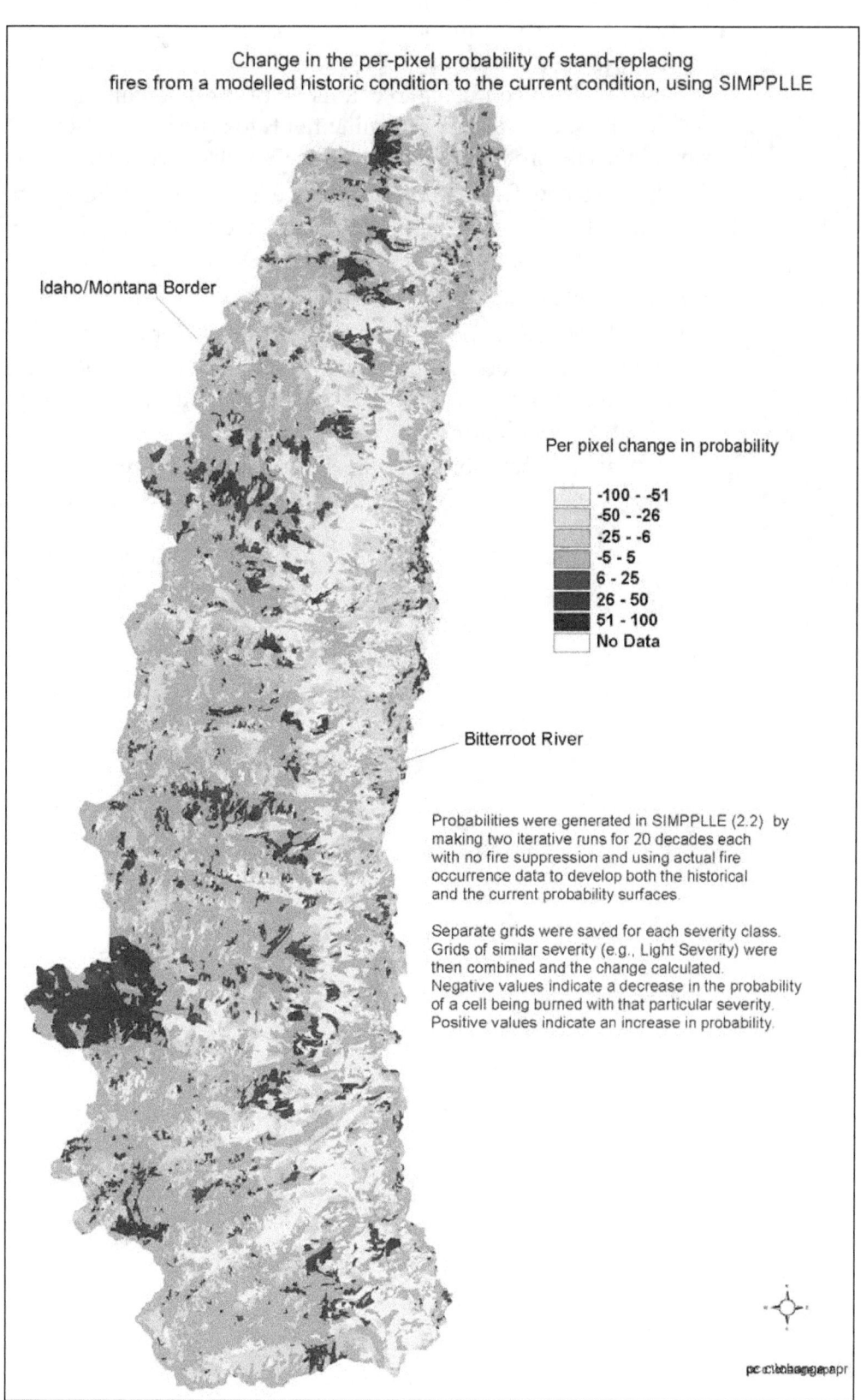

Change in the per-pixel probability of stand-replacing
fires from a modelled historic condition to the current condition, using SIMPPLLE

Idaho/Montana Border

Per pixel change in probability

-100 - -51
-50 - -26
-25 - -6
-5 - 5
6 - 25
26 - 50
51 - 100
No Data

Bitterroot River

Probabilities were generated in SIMPPLLE (2.2) by
making two iterative runs for 20 decades each
with no fire suppression and using actual fire
occurrence data to develop both the historical
and the current probability surfaces.

Separate grids were saved for each severity class.
Grids of similar severity (e.g., Light Severity) were
then combined and the change calculated.
Negative values indicate a decrease in the probability
of a cell being burned with that particular severity.
Positive values indicate an increase in probability.

Figure 21 - Example map of change in probability of Stand Replacing Fire.

2. Compare most likely fire type.

2.1. *Join* the fire portions of the *–n-process.txt* files to the SIMPPLLE coverage (or use SIMPPLLE's ARCVIEW extension to do this for you). We found it least confusing to edit the .txt files first, eliminating all but the relevant fields and renaming fields to reflect the different simulations before joining the file to the SIMPPLLE coverage.

2.1.a. Add a new field to identify change in fire type and develop a classification of change. We found three general types of change: no change, more/less severe, more/less variable.

2.1.b. Develop a rule-set for classifying change.

2.1.c. Subtract one severity class from the other (for example, subtracting historic from current results in negatives for decreases and positive number for increases in probability). It is easiest to hide fields not in use.

2.2. Map change in probability of fire severity class (**Figure 22**).

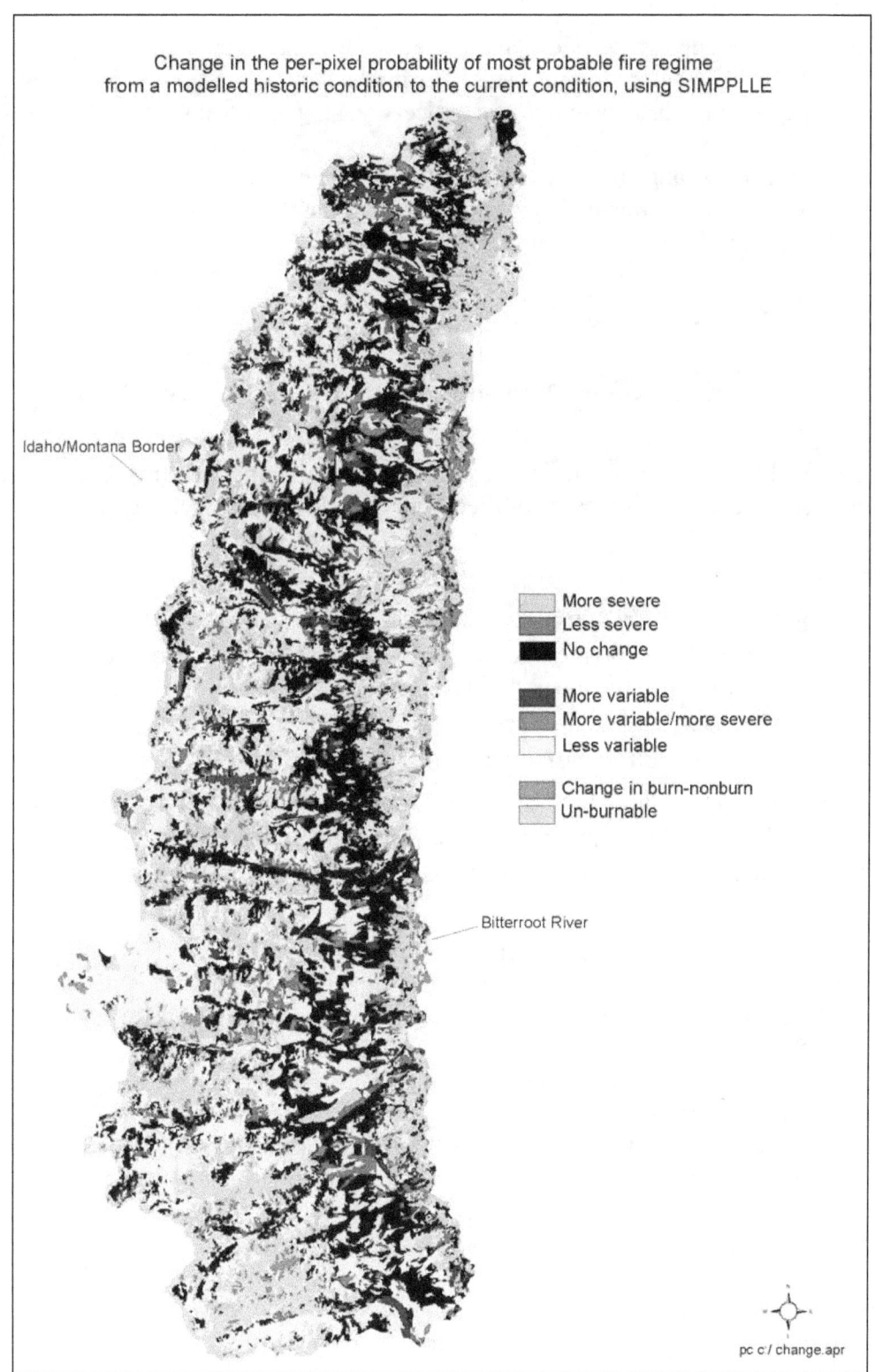

Change in the per-pixel probability of most probable fire regime
from a modelled historic condition to the current condition, using SIMPPLLE

Idaho/Montana Border

More severe
Less severe
No change

More variable
More variable/more severe
Less variable

Change in burn-nonburn
Un-burnable

Bitterroot River

pc c:/ change.apr

Figure 22 - Example map of change in most probable fire type using SIMPPLLE output.

Chapter 3. Using map libraries

FEPF map libraries support decisions at all stages of fire management planning. This sets the stage for identifying opportunities and risks in the coming season(s). Here, we outline potential analyses, then provide examples of decision support documents to:

- Support long-range management plan development;
- Support identification of fuels treatment priorities; and
- Support fire stewardship activities.

Support Long-range Management Plan Development

FEPF can facilitate fire management by assisting in establishing the range of acceptable appropriate management responses codified in the Land/Resource Management plan.

Potential Analyses
1. Support for long-range plan development
    1.1. Run analyses for alternatives to determine feasibility, consequences, and opportunities for fire and fuels management. Compare fire probability and most likely fire type across time or management alternatives.
2. Support for plan implementation
    2.1. Run a comparison between the current situation and ecological targets.
    2.2. Identify alternative treatment strategies and conduct runs to determine feasibility, consequences, and opportunities for meeting targets.

At the broad-scale, FEPF generates maps and criteria for determining feasibility, consequences, and opportunities for fire and fuels management. In our demonstrations with the Bitterroot National Forest, we used two combinations of SIMMPLLE and FLAMMAP to compare the landscape level effects of treating stands 'at risk'. A key management concern for the Bitterroot National Forest is the restoration of fire to fire-adapted cover types. We identified these cover types as stands of fire tolerant species of ponderosa pine, Douglas-fir, and western larch. Stands 'at risk' are those with sufficient stem density to carry a stand-replacing crown fire under even moderate fire weather conditions. For both analyses, we used SIMPPLLE and FLAMMAP runs on the current landscape condition to identify early seral stands (though not necessarily young stands) currently 'at risk' from fire.

These analyses help managers and the public understand the opportunities, consequences, and feasibility of various land, fuel, and fire management strategies.

Using SIMPPLLE to compare probable burn type We programmed SIMPPLLE to treat the identified stands with a combination mechanical treatment followed by a broadcast underburn (ecosystem management thin and underburn). Treatments were intended to restore the stands to more historically natural conditions that support a surface fire but not a crown fire.

We then ran a single decade SIMPPLLE simulation on the existing and the treated landscapes, using 30 iterations for each to capture ecosystem variability. We calculated the most probable fire type (light, mixed, or stand-replacing fire) for each stand in each simulation from the SIMPPLLE output files. Most probable burn type maps were translated into fire effects maps using a rule-based crosswalk. These final effects maps identify where fire is likely to produce uncharacteristic (risk) or characteristic (benefit or opportunity) effects (**Figure 23**). If we were to do this for several treatment strategies, we could then quantify the difference between the alternatives and identify how each would affect the Forest's ability to meet its target.

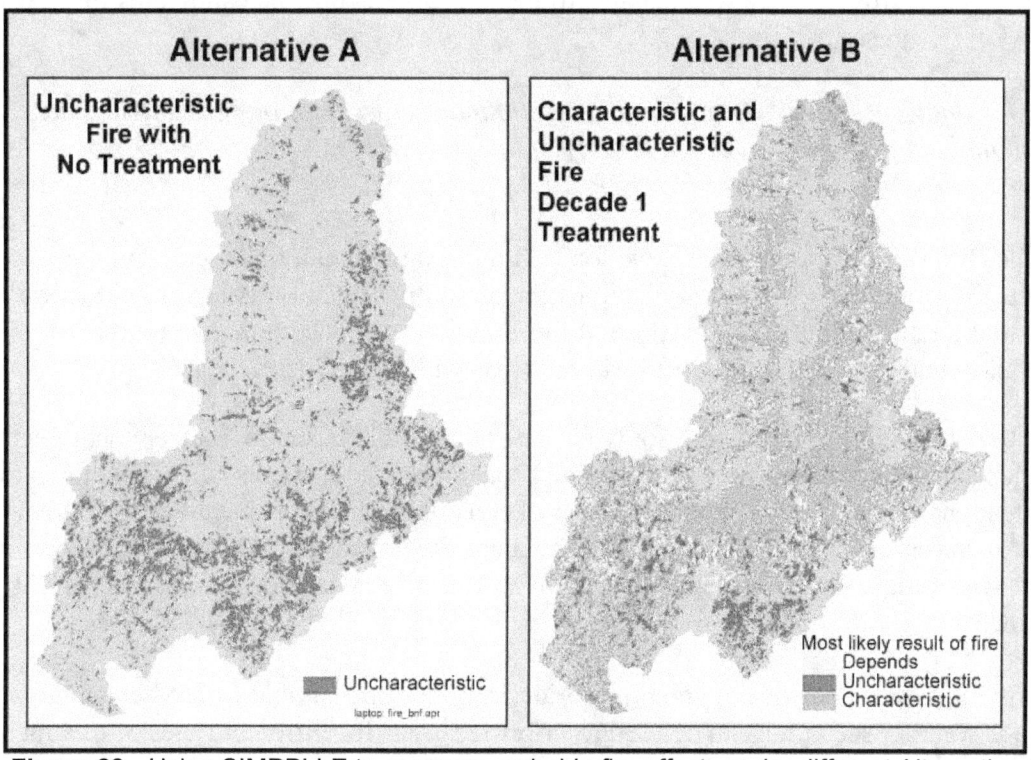

Figure 23 - Using SIMPPLLE to compare probable fire effects under different Alternatives.

Using FLAMMAP to compare fire type Alternatively, if one desires to use a quantitative measure of fire behavior, it is possible to use SIMPPLLE to generate the future landscape, apply a crosswalk from SIMPPLLE vegetation composition and structure to fuel model and canopy fuels for both the existing and future landscapes, and use FLAMMAP to predict fire behavior parameters for both situations. This combination can produce comparisons of fire behavior parameters, such as flame length or rate of spread, as well as fire type (surface, passive crown fire, active crown fire).

Support Identification of Fuels Treatment Priorities

Potential Analyses

1. Query across the threshold fire effects maps to identify areas that
   are consistently:
   a) <u>characteristic or desirable</u>. These areas are candidates for reintroduction of
      fire.
   b) <u>uncharacteristic or undesirable</u>. These areas (or areas with their attributes)
      are candidates for mechanical treatment.
   c) <u>variable</u>. Fire behavior and/or effects vary in character and/or desirability
      across the fire weather spectrum. These areas may be candidates for
      prescribed fire.

   This analysis should be considered a preliminary classification. Field assessment
   should always follow to check validity of the model runs.

On the Bitterroot National Forest, we focused this example at a finer scale, on the
Bitterroot Front, using our Fire Behavior Library (output from FLAMMAP) to identify
potential treatment units. The purpose of this simulation was to demonstrate the
feasibility and potential utility of FEPF, not to provide actual data.

We combined the fire effects grids for lynx (for example, all percentile weather conditions) to
develop a map indicating where fire under all situations creates benefits, and where fire under
all situations creates risks (**Figure 24**). Areas of consistent benefit are candidates for fire use;
areas of consistent risk are candidates for mechanical treatments prior to reintroduction of fire.
Areas with variable effects can be further analyzed for either prescribed fire or mechanical
treatments.

Information on the consistent potential for desirable or undesirable fire effects under
various weather scenarios can be used to prioritize areas for different types of treatment
(wildland fire use, mechanical, or prescribed fire). Treatment unit boundaries or
ecological units (for example lynx analysis units, or LAUs) can be added to the GIS and
analyzed using the desirable/undesirable frequency data. This GIS table can be sorted
and exported to essentially create a prioritized treatment list.

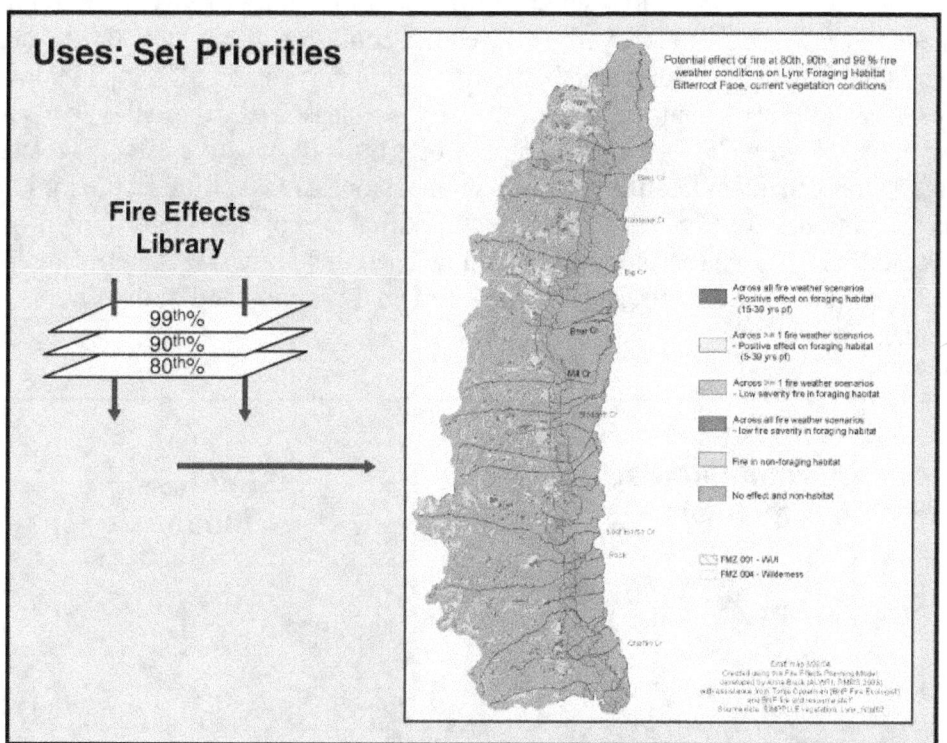

Figure 24 - Illustration of how to query a fire behavior library to determine treatment priorities.

Support Fire Stewardship Activities

Fire Plan Development

Map layers can be used during creation or revision of Fire Management Plans to:
- identify resources values, objectives/desired conditions/standards and guides, and constraints for each management/response unit;
- pre-plan Fire Management or Maximum Manageable Areas; and
- aid in determining appropriate prescriptions, boundaries, and priorities for management-ignited prescribed fires.

Either SIMPPLLE or FLAMMAP can be used for this purpose.

Potential Analyses

1. Use the difference between ecological targets and existing condition to identify alternative fire/fuel management strategies –such as expanded WFU zones.

2. Test these potential strategies by running multiple simulations and checking the results against ecological (and social) targets.

In one exercise, we identified potential WFU zones by calculating the percentage of each subwatershed (6th HUC) in (a) low severity fire under moderate fire weather conditions and (b) active crown fire under severe fire weather conditions from FLAMMAP output for the Bitterroot River valley. Subwatersheds with a high percentage of lands in a low severity class and low percentage in high severity we classed as candidates for Wildland Fire Use zones (**Figure 25**). Areas with high proportions of negative effects we classed as candidates for mechanical treatment and/or suppression. Areas falling in the middle can either be conditional WFU zones and/or used to define appropriate conditions for prescribed burns. These subwatersheds could be used to summarize benefits and risks from the map library, with the resulting maps and analysis included in the Fire Management Plan.

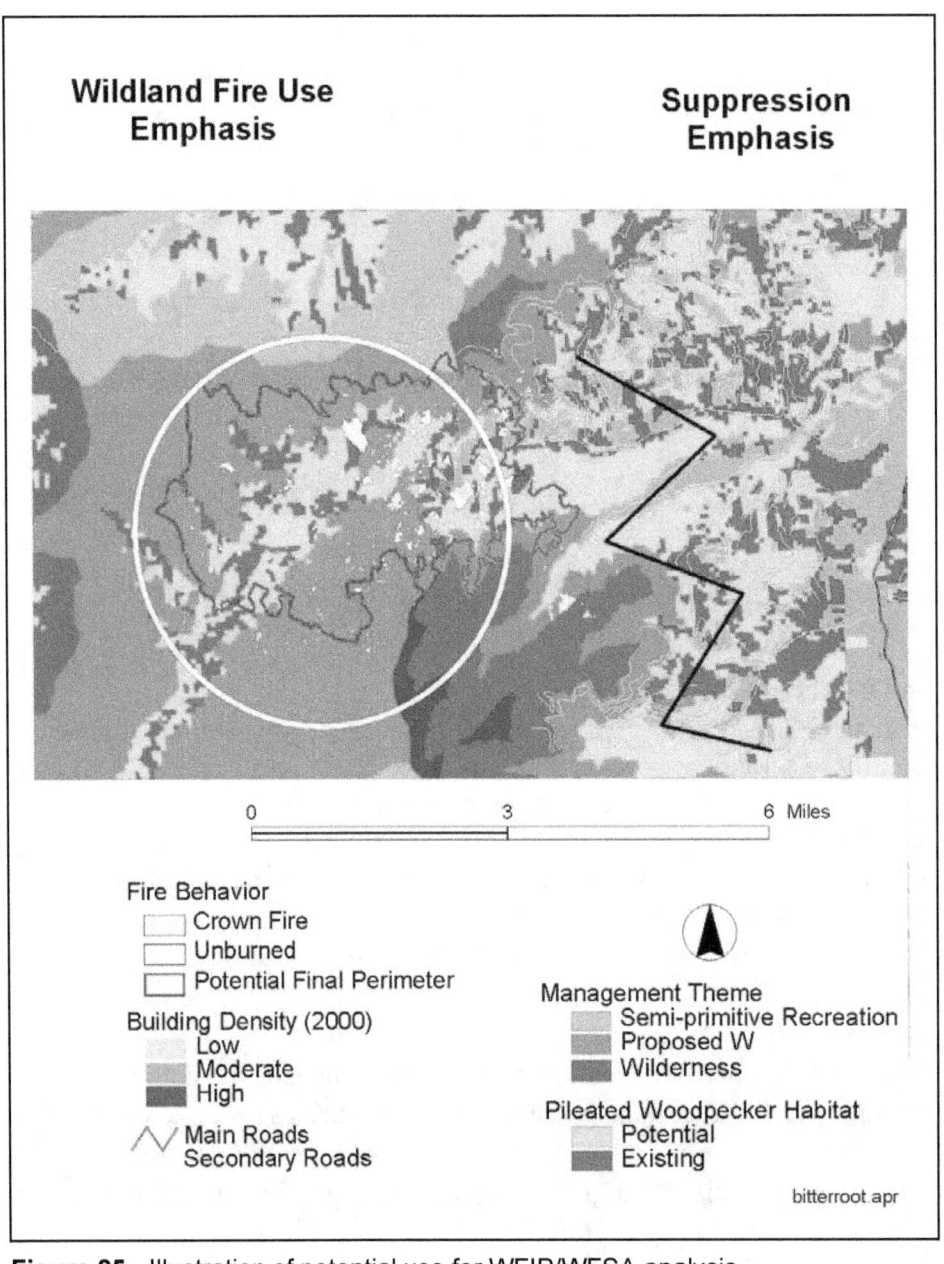

Figure 25 - Illustration of potential use for WFIP/WFSA analysis.

Fire Season Planning

Areas identified during fuels treatment prioritization efforts can be rolled into annual activity plans, particularly areas where Wildland Fire Use and prescribed fire are the most ecologically, economically and socially feasible options. When considered in light of other resources values, values at risk, and potential for a natural ignition, these maps can be used to prioritize annual management activities.

Potential Analyses

1. Determine areas where natural fires, under various fire weather conditions, might be managed for Wildland Fire Use. Determine areas where fire, under various fire weather conditions, poses unacceptable risks.
2. Use this information to develop spring-fall fuels management activities.

Incident Management and Cost Containment

FEPF output can be used at each planning step mandated in the federal *Wildland and Prescribed Fire Management Policy - – Implementation Procedures Reference Guide*, published by the NIFC (National Interagency Fire Center) in August 1998.

Potential Analyses

Map libraries of fire effects provide important information for incident support.

1. Overlay predicted fire perimeters on predicted effects maps for the threshold conditions closest to existing conditions to determine spatial location of benefits and risks.
2. Identify and quantify non-monetary benefits and changes to management targets using the GIS database and integrate this information into the various fire management decision documents.

The fire effects map library can be used to develop tactical plans, taking advantage of where fire may be used to achieve resource benefits. Because fire use is generally much cheaper than aggressive suppression efforts, taking advantage of information contained in map libraries can contribute to cost containment. The Appropriate Management Response includes the full range of management options from full, aggressive suppression to Wildland Fire Use. FEPF can provide spatial and tabular summaries of opportunities under a gamut of fire weather threshold conditions. Information on potential benefits under threshold conditions closest to the expected weather can be weighed along with effects on other values and values at risk during the initial "go/no go" decision stage. If Wildland Fire Use is the chosen strategy, development of WFIP Stage II and III reports are informed through the FEPF process as well.

Finally, pre-developed map layers identifying areas of ecological benefit and risk can be useful in developing and prioritizing fire suppression activities. Spatial identification of potential benefits can help management teams target areas to contain or confine strategies instead of employing the generally more resource intensive control tactics. Map layers may also be indispensable for teams unfamiliar with the fire area or ecology.

III. Forms

NOTE: these forms are available as two Excel files, but are provided here for illustration and hard copy use.

1. Weather Form (for capturing critical weather data from FIREFAMILYPLUS)

2. Tracking sheet for FLAMMAP runs.

3. Run_template.xls (for assessing and capturing adjustments to critical SIMPPLLE logic tables).
   3.1 System Knowledge
   3.2 Simulations
   3.3 Import/export
   3.4 Reports
   3.5 Knowledge files
       a. *Fire occurrence (FMZ)*
       b. *Class A*
       c. *beyondclassA*
       d. *firesuppweathera*
       e. *firesuppweather*
       f. *extreme fire prob*
       g. *regional climate*
       h. *Type of Fire Logic*

Form 2.

FlamMap

FlamMap

INPUTS
Run Name _____ *.lcp _____

Fuel Moisture Files
_____ *.fms
_____ *.fmd

Winds
Uphill _____   20' wind= _____
Direction _____   Azimuth= _____

Canopy
LiveFM% _____

Fuel Moisture Settings
Fixed _____
Conditioning _____

Conditioning Period   Start Date/Time _____
End Date/Time _____

OUTPUTS
Threading: Multiple   Single

Output Grids
_____ *.fli
_____ *.ros
_____ *.fml
_____ *.hpa
_____ *.cfr
_____ *.rhm

Spread Direction: Relative Absolute (degrees _____)

FlamMap

INPUTS
Run Name _____ *.lcp _____

Fuel Moisture Files
_____ *.fms
_____ *.fmd

Winds
Uphill _____   20' wind= _____
Direction _____   Azimuth= _____

Canopy
LiveFM% _____

Fuel Moisture Settings
Fixed _____
Conditioning _____

Conditioning Period   Start Date/Time _____
End Date/Time _____

OUTPUTS
Threading: Multiple   Single

Output Grids
_____ *.fli
_____ *.ros
_____ *.fml
_____ *.hpa
_____ *.cfr
_____ *.rhm

Spread Direction: Relative Absolute (degrees _____)

FlamMap

INPUTS
Run Name _____ *.lcp _____

Fuel Moisture Files
_____ *.fms
_____ *.fmd

Winds
Uphill _____   20' wind= _____
Direction _____   Azimuth= _____

Canopy
LiveFM% _____

Fuel Moisture Settings
Fixed _____
Conditioning _____

Conditioning Period   Start Date/Time _____
End Date/Time _____

OUTPUTS
Threading: Multiple   Single

Output Grids
_____ *.fli
_____ *.ros
_____ *.fml
_____ *.hpa
_____ *.cfr
_____ *.rhm

Spread Direction: Relative Absolute (degrees _____)

Form 2.

FlamMap

FlamMap

INPUTS
Run Name _____
_____ *.lcp

Fuel Moisture Files
_____ *.fms
_____ *.fmd

Winds
Uphill _____ 20' wind= _____
Direction _____ Azimuth= _____

Canopy
LiveFM% _____

Fuel Moisture Settings
Fixed _____
Conditioning _____

Conditioning Period Start Date/Time _____
End Date/Time _____

OUTPUTS
Threading: Multiple   Single

Output Grids
_____ *.fli
_____ *.ros
_____ *.fml
_____ *.hpa
_____ *.cfr
_____ *.rhm

Spread Direction: Relative   Absolute (degrees _____)

FlamMap

INPUTS
Run Name _____
_____ *.lcp

Fuel Moisture Files
_____ *.fms
_____ *.fmd

Winds
Uphill _____ 20' wind= _____
Direction _____ Azimuth= _____

Canopy
LiveFM% _____

Fuel Moisture Settings
Fixed _____
Conditioning _____

Conditioning Period Start Date/Time _____
End Date/Time _____

OUTPUTS
Threading: Multiple   Single

Output Grids
_____ *.fli
_____ *.ros
_____ *.fml
_____ *.hpa
_____ *.cfr
_____ *.rhm

Spread Direction: Relative   Absolute (degrees _____)

FlamMap

INPUTS
Run Name _____
_____ *.lcp

Fuel Moisture Files
_____ *.fms
_____ *.fmd

Winds
Uphill _____ 20' wind= _____
Direction _____ Azimuth= _____

Canopy
LiveFM% _____

Fuel Moisture Settings
Fixed _____
Conditioning _____

Conditioning Period Start Date/Time _____
End Date/Time _____

OUTPUTS
Threading: Multiple   Single

Output Grids
_____ *.fli
_____ *.ros
_____ *.fml
_____ *.hpa
_____ *.cfr
_____ *.rhm

Spread Direction: Relative   Absolute (degrees _____)

FORM 3.1

System Knowledge

Work Area:

Team:

Zone

Area

System Knowledge

INPUT OPTIONS				File extension	Storage file name	Parameters	Source Data
Pathways							
	Vegetative			.pathway			
	Aquatic			n/a at this time			
Vegetation processes							
	Lockin processes			.process			
	Fire spread			.firespread			
	Extreme fire spread prob						
	Fire suppression cost			fmz			
	Fire occurrence input			fmz			
	Fire suppression logic						
		Class A		firesupression			
		Beyond Class A		.firesuppbeyonda			
	Type of fire logic			.firetype			
	Weather ending events						
		< 0.25 acre		.firesuppweathera			
		> 0.25 acre		.firesuppweather			
	WSBW logic			n/a at this time			
	Insect/Disease logic			n/a at this time			
	Insect/disease occurrence prob			.probability			
	Use regen pulse (Y/N)						
	Regen			n/a at this time			
	Weed spread			n/a at this time			
	Conifer encroachment			n/a at this time			
Aquatic processes				n/a at this time			
Vegetative Treatments							
	Treatment schedule			.treatment			
	Treatment logic			.treatmentlogic			
Aquatic treatments							
Regional Climate				.climate			
System Knowledge				.sysknowledge			

SMPPLEE_forms.xls

Form 3.2

Simulations

Work Area:						
Team:						
Zone						
Area						
SIMPPLLE simulation	.area file/landscape file	Storage area	Timestep (1,10)	# steps	# iterations	
Name						

Form 3.3 Import/Export

Work Area:					
Team:					
		OPTIONS	File extension	Storage file name	Parameters	Source Data
Zone						
Area						
	Import	run neighbors	.nbr			
		create new area	.area			
		load attributes	.attributes			
	Export	GIS Simulation Files				
		spread				
		accumulation				
		probability by decade				
		probability of reburn				
		Attributes	.attributes			

Form 3.4 Reports

Work Area:							
Team:							
Zone							
Area							

Form 3.5a

Fire Occurrence

	FMZ			1			2			3			4		
	all														
Acres	Lightning	Human	$/Acre	Lightning	Human	$/Acre	Lightning	Human	$/Acre	Lightning	Human	$/Acre	Lightning	Human	$/Acre
0.00 - 0.25															
0.26 - 9.99															
10.00 - 99.99															
100.0 - 299.99															
300.00 - 999.99															
1000.00+															

SIMPPLLE file name:

Source files:

Form 3.5c - 3.5g

Fire Information

Form 3.5c — Beyond Class A Fire

Process	Ownership (choose to suppress)		Roads Status (Choose to limit suppression)		
SRF	NF Wilderness	x			
	NF Other	x	open-roaded	closed-roaded	none
	Other	x	open-roaded	closed-roaded	none
MSF	NF Wilderness	x			
	NF Other	x	open-roaded	closed-roaded	none
	Other	x	open-roaded	closed-roaded	none
LSF	NF Wilderness	x			
	NF Other	x	open-roaded	closed-roaded	none
	Other	x	open-roaded	closed-roaded	none

SIMPPLLE file name: DEFAULT

Form 3.5d — Fire Suppression Weather a

species	wetter	normal	drier
a	50	25	0
b	25	0	0

SIMPPLLE file name: defaults

Form 3.5e — Fire Suppression Weather

Size	Event Probability
0.25 - 500	0
501 - 1000	10
1001 - 5000	25
5001 - 10000	35
10001 - 50000	50
50000+	75

SIMPPLLE file name: default

Form 3.f — Extreme Fire Probability

	Default
Probability due to weather event	0
Fire event acres for 100% probability	1000

Form 3.5g — Regional Climate

timestep	1	2	3	4	5
Temp					
Moisture					

Form 3.5h   Type of Fire Logic

Size/Structure	Resistance	Size Class	Density	Past Treatment	Past Process	Regional Climate		
defaults for bitterroot - june 2003						wetter	normal	drier
Non-Forest	low	all	1,2,3,4			SRF	SRF	SRF
	moderate		1,2			MSF	MSF	MSF
			3,4			SRF	SRF	SRF
	high	scatt, clump,op	1,2			LSF	LSF	LSF
		scat, clump ope	3,4			LSF	MSF	SRF
		uniform, closed	1,2,3,4			MSF	SRF	SRF
		open shrub typ	1,2,3,4			LSF	MSF	MSF
Single Story	low	ss	1,2	EMBroad, PCT		LSF	LSF	MSF
			3,4	all others		MSF	SRF	SRF
			1,2,3,4	no match		MSF	SRF	SRF
		pole	1,2	EMBroad, PCT		LSF	LSF	MSF
			3,4	all others		MSF	SRF	SRF
			1,2,3,4	no match		MSF	SRF	SRF
		m, l, vl	1,2	EMU, EMTU	LSF, MSF root, s-wsbw, pp-mpb, s-lp-mpb	LSF	LSF	MSF
			1,2,3,4	all others		LSF	MSF	SRF
			1,2,3,4	no match		MSF	SRF	SRF
	moderate	ss	1,2	EMBroad, PCT		LSF	LSF	MSF
			3,4	all others		LSF	MSF	SRF
			1,2,3,4	no match		MSF	MSF	MSF
		pole	1,2	EMBroad, PCT		LSF	LSF	MSF
			3,4	all others		LSF	MSF	SRF
			1,2,3,4	no match		LSF	MSF	MSF
		m, l, vl	1,2	EMU, EMTU	LSF, MSF root, s-wsbw, pp-mpb, s-lp-mpb	LSF	LSF	LSF
			1,2,3,4	all others		MSF	MSF	SRF
			1,2,3,4	no match		LSF	MSF	MSF
	high	ss	1,2	EMB, PCT		LSF	LSF	LSF
			3,4	EMB, PCT		MSF	MSF	MSF
			3,4	all others		MSF	MSF	MSF
			1,2	no match		LSF	LSF	LSF
			3,4	no match		LSF	MSF	SRF
		pole	1,2	EMB, PCT		LSF	LSF	LSF
			3,4	EMB, PCT		MSF	MSF	MSF
			3,4	all others		MSF	MSF	MSF
			1,2	no match		LSF	LSF	LSF
			3,4	no match		LSF	MSF	SRF
		m, l, vl	1,2,3,4	EMB, TMTU		LSF	LSF	LSF
			1,2	all others		MSF	MSF	MSF
			3,4	all others		SRF	MSF	SRF
			1,2,3,4	no match		MSF	LSF	LSF
Multi-story	low	all	1,2	EMU, EMTU		LSF	LSF	MSF
			1,2,3,4	all others	root disease	MSF	MSF	SRF
			1,2,3,4	no match		MSF	SRF	SRF
	moderate	all	1,2	EMU, EMTU		LSF	LSF	LSF
			1,2,3,4	all others	root disease	LSF	MSF	SRF
			1,2,3,4	no match		LSF	MSF	MSF
	high	all	1,2	EMU, EMTU		LSF	LSF	LSF
			1,2	all others	root disease	LSF	MSF	MSF
			3,4	all others	root disease	LSF	MSF	SRF
			1,2,3,4	no match		LSF	MSF	MSF

SIMPPLLE file name: revised default - new_bttr.firetype

References

Albini, F.A. 1976. Estimating wildfire behavior and effects. GTR-INT-30. Ogden, UT: U.S. Department of Agriculture, Forest Service, Intermountain Research Station.

Barrett, T.M. 2001. Models of vegetative change for landscape planning: a comparison of FETM, LANDSUM, SIMPPLLE, and VDDT. RMRS-GTR-76WWW. Fort Collins, CO: U.S. Department of Agriculture, Forest Service, Rocky Mountain Research Station.

Bradshaw, L., McCormick, E. 2000. FireFamilyPlus user's guide, version 2.0. RMRS-GTR-67WWW. Ogden, UT: U.S. Department of Agriculture, Forest Service, Rocky Mountain Research Station.

Chew, J.D. 1995. Development of a system for simulating vegetative patterns and processes at landscape scales. PhD Dissertation. University of Montana, Missoula.

Chew, J.D., Stalling, C., Moeller, K. 2004. Integrating knowledge for simulating vegetation change at landscape scales. *Western Journal of Applied Forestry.* 19(Part 2):102-108.

DeBano, L.F., Neary, D.G., Ffolliott, P.F. 1998. Fire's effects on ecosystems. John Wiley & Sons, Inc. 333 p.

Finney, M.A. 1994. Modeling the spread and behavior of prescribed natural fires. In: Proceedings of the 12th conference on fire and forest meteorology; 1993 October 26-28; Jekyll Is. GA. Society of American Publishers:138-143.

Finney, M.A. [in preparation]. FlamMap. Missoula, MT: U.S. Department of Agriculture, Forest Service, Rocky Mountain Research Station, Fire Sciences Laboratory.

Lee, B., Meneghin, M., Turner, M., Hoekstra, T. 2003. An evaluation of landscape dynamic simulation models. Internal review by the Inventory and Monitoring Institute. Fort Collins, CO: U.S. Department of Agriculture, Forest Service, Rocky Mountain Research Station.

Miller, C., Landres, P.B., Alaback, P.B. 2000. Evaluating the risks and benefits of wildland fire at landscape scales. In: Neuenschwander, L.F., Ryan K.C. (tech. eds.):Joint Fire Science Conference and Workshop: proceedings; 1999 June 15-17; Boise, ID. Moscow, ID:University of Idaho:78-87.

Rothermel, R.C. 1972. A mathematical model for predicting fire spread in wildland fuels. Research Paper INT-115. Ogden, UT: U.S. Department of Agriculture, Forest Service, Intermountain Research Station.

Ruediger, B., Claar, J., Gniadek, S., Holt, B., Lewis, L., Mighton, S., Naney, B., Patton, G., Rinaldi, T., Trick, J., Vandehey, A., Wahl, F., Warren, N., Wenger, D., Williamson, A. 2000. Canada lynx conservation assessment and strategy. U.S.Department of Agriculture Forest Service, U.S. Departments of Interior: Fish and Wildlife Service, Bureau of Land Management, National Park Service, Missoula, MT.

RMRS

ROCKY MOUNTAIN RESEARCH STATION

The Rocky Mountain Research Station develops scientific information and technology to improve management, protection, and use of the forests and rangelands. Research is designed to meet the needs of the National Forest managers, Federal and State agencies, public and private organizations, academic institutions, industry, and individuals.

Studies accelerate solutions to problems involving ecosystems, range, forests, water, recreation, fire, resource inventory, land reclamation, community sustainability, forest engineering technology, multiple use economics, wildlife and fish habitat, and forest insects and diseases. Studies are conducted cooperatively, and applications may be found worldwide.

Research Locations

Flagstaff, Arizona	Reno, Nevada
Fort Collins, Colorado*	Albuquerque, New Mexico
Boise, Idaho	Rapid City, South Dakota
Moscow, Idaho	Logan, Utah
Bozeman, Montana	Ogden, Utah
Missoula, Montana	Provo, Utah

*Station Headquarters, Natural Resources Research Center, 2150 Centre Avenue, Building A, Fort Collins, CO 80526.